S0-BFB-608

WYOMING MOUNTAIN RANGES

Text © 1987 by Lorraine G. Bonney

NUMBER ONE

Wyoming
Geographic
Series

AMERICAN GEOGRAPHIC PUBLISHING

WILLIAM A. CORDINGLEY, CHAIRMAN
RICK GRAETZ, PUBLISHER
MARK THOMPSON, DIRECTOR OF PUBLICATIONS
BARBARA FIFER, ASSISTANT BOOK EDITOR

This series provides in-depth information about Wyoming's geographical, natural history, historical and cultural subjects. Design by Len Visual Design. Printed in Hong Kong by DNP America, Inc., San Francisco.

Left: In the Wind River Range.
CHARLES PHILLIPS
Right: Clarks Fork Canyon.
GEORGE WUERTHNER

Cover photos, clockwise from left:
The Tetons from Grand Targhee.
NEAL ROGERS
Alpine sunflowers, Cirque of the Towers, Wind River Range.
JEFF GNASS
Cougar. LEONARD LEE RUE III
Aerial view, looking south, in Grand Teton National Park.
PAT O'HARA

ISBN 0-938314-27-0

published by
American Geographic Publishing
P.O. Box 5630
Helena, Montana 59604

Mammoth
Mt. Washburn
BEARTOOTH MTNS.
West Yellowstone
Yellowstone National Yellowstone Park
Yellowstone Lake
Sheridan
Cody
Hallalujah Peak
Black Tooth Peak
Sawtooth Peak · Penrose Peak
Cloud Peak
Buffalo
Missouri Buttes
Devils Tower
BEAR LODGE MTNS.
GALLATIN RANGE
ABSAROKA RANGE
RED MTNS
Mt. Sheridan
TETON RANGE
WASHAKIE RANGE
Younts Peak
Ramshorn Peak
Francs Peak
BIGHORN RANGE
Bighorn River
Powder River
Belle Fourche River
Mt. Moran
Grand Teton
Mt. Leidy
Sheep Mtn.
Kelly
Pinnacle Buttes
Washakie Needles
Thermopolis
OWL CREEK RANGE
Gros Ventre Slide
Dubois
Phlox Mtn.
GROS VENTRE RANGE
Powder Peak
Jackson
Whiskey Peak
Wind River Indian Reservation
SNAKE R. RANGE
Battle Mountain
Gannett Peak
Dinwoody Glacier
WIND RIVER
Shoshoni
Mt. Woodrow Wilson
Riverton
Mt. Bonneville
SALT R. RANGE
Grayback Ridge
WYOMING RANGE
Cirque of the Towers
Lander
RANGE
Rock Lake Peak
Star Valley
Wind River Peak
Lonesome Lake
Continental Divide
Garfield Peak
RATTLESNAKE HILLS
North Platte River
Casper
Casper Mountain
Oregon Trail
Commissary Ridge
South Pass
Sweetwater River
GRANITE MTN.
Split Rock
Devils Gate
Independence Rock
FERRIS MTNS.
SEMINOE MTNS.
SHIRLEY MTNS.
Oregon Buttes
Continental Peak
Continental Divide
GREEN MTN.
Ferris Dune Field
Bradley Peak
BENNETT MTNS.
Fossil Butte National Monument
Kemmerer
LEUCITE HILLS
Killpecker Dunes
GREAT DIVIDE BASIN (RED DESERT)
RAWLINS UPLIFT
Rawlins
LARAMIE RANGE
Green River
Rock Springs
Divide
Bridger Pass
SIERRA MADRE RANGE
SNOWY RANGE
MEDICINE BOW MTNS.
Medicine Bow Peak
Laramie
Veedauwoo Rocks
The Gangplank
Cheyenne
SHERMAN MTNS.
Evanston

2

PREFACE

Wyoming, from the Leni Lenape Indian word Maughwauwama meaning "undulating plains and mountains."

Wyoming, the Cowboy State. A state so renowned for its scenic grandeur, unsurpassed wildlife and vast wild lands that it has been described as "the Alaska of the Lower 48 States." Indeed, that unique area of the nation, the Greater Yellowstone Ecosystem, which fills the northwest corner of Wyoming, is the largest block of wild land in the country outside of Alaska.

Wyoming. The site of the first national park (Yellowstone), the first national monument (Devils Tower), and the first national forest (Shoshone).

Wyoming. The home of the largest elk, bighorn sheep, bison and pronghorn antelope herds in the world. Where there are more big-game animals than people. A state that still has room for such threatened species as the grizzly bear, the peregrine falcon, the trumpeter swan, and the black-footed ferret.

Wyoming. Where that living metaphor for courage, freedom and honor, the golden eagle—once almost lost, now back—represents the best in the wild.

Wyoming. Its high mountain lakes and streams provide blue-ribbon trout fishing and serve as the fountainhead for the West's mightiest rivers—the Columbia, the Missouri and the Colorado.

Wyoming. Its mountains were pilot guides to the Astorians, sacred altars for the Indian, the last hideouts for Indians and outlaws alike.

Wyoming. Whose citizens are the caretakers of that which has disappeared from the rest of this nation.

Wyoming. Half Rocky Mountain cordillera, half Great American Desert. Where every geologic period in the history of the earth is represented.

Mount Moran, Grand Teton National Park, with Jackson Lake and balsamroot. PAT O'HARA

Wyoming's magic appeal of national attractions—spectacular mountains, rumbling hot spots of still-active crustal deformation, great sagebrush deserts covering trapped minerals, glacier age-sand dunes, miles of fascinating wilderness—can be divided into three geological provinces. There are the mountain cores of Precambrian crystalline rock; then the volcanic area of Yellowstone National Park, the Absaroka Range, and other isolated areas in the Black Hills, Rattlesnake Hills, Leucite Hills and Devils Tower; and finally the basin areas layered with centuries of sedimentary rocks and anticline folds of trapped mineral wealth.

Whence came all this wealth? The Wyoming landscape tells a story of drifting continents, colliding continental plates, earth-shattering crustal movements and volcanic hot spots. Come join us for a quick tour!

CONTENTS

GEOLOGY

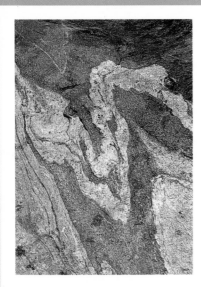

The banded Precambrian gneisses and granites of the Tetons.
GRAND TETON NATIONAL PARK

The Teton Range from Snake River Overlook. This faulted range has no foothills. The Tetons, youngest of Wyoming mountain ranges, are composed of rocks that record seven eighths of all geologic time— Precambrian gneisses and granites. PAT O'HARA

4

The Basement Rocks

Of the four great geologic eras that contributed to the tempering and shaping of Wyoming's exceptional landscape, the first and longest, the Precambrian, lasted some 4 billion years, taking up seven eighths of the yardstick of geologic time, 90 percent of the earth's history. Any clues concerning the events that created this foundation rock of our North American continent, perhaps its very birth, have been scattered, buried, disrupted in the mists of time by later cataclysmic events, so that piecing together the Precambrian story is like trying to read the history of an ancient and long-forgotten civilization from the scattered unnumbered pages of a torn manuscript, written in a language that is only partially understood.

The ancient layered gneisses and schists of Precambrian rocks, exposed in the cores of most Wyoming mountain ranges, were formed of very thick sedimentary and volcanic rocks that were folded and metamorphosed (radically changed by high temperatures and pressures into "new" minerals), and intruded upon by other rock types like granites, pegmatites and basalts. They are the up-rooted "roots" of numerous series of long-gone ancestral ranges that arose and fell during 2,000 million years, a passing parade of big mountains violently developed, then wiped out, worn down by erosion until the land surface was reduced to a nearly featureless plain, a peneplane.

The Age of Seas

With only one eighth of geology's yardstick of time left to accomplish the shaping of a continent and a state, the second great era, the Paleozoic, 375 million years of seas, undoubtedly presented the wettest, flattest landscape of all as shallow, warm-water inland seas invaded and retreated again and again across the vast flatness that was Wyoming, leaving behind crusty layers of limestone and sandstone. Some of these marine transgressions coincided with the great ocean upheavals that occurred when intense seafloor spreading and lifting displaced great amounts of water, and ocean levels rose inundating much of North America and other continents.

As centuries of seas, often shallow and warm, lapped against Wyoming's long-vanished beaches, ancient sea bottoms of mud and sand settled into vast sedimentary layers littered with the dead bodies of nature's early experiments with life. From the bizarre to the beautiful, suc-

cesses and failures were fully preserved in an excellent fossil record of the oldest fish remains—vertebrate fossils—known in geological history. After the seas reached their maximum extent they took another 200 million years slowly to retreat both eastward and westward, leaving the inland basins filled with dead marine organisms, Wyoming's future oil deposits.

The 160-million-year Mesozoic era was a time of transition as the restless water-soaked landscape dried out. Living among marine, transitional and continental environments, its highly diversified life forms ranged from sea mollusks to dinosaurs. With the environment shifting back and forth between wet and dry, living things were forced to move from sea to land to survive.

After 500 million years of Paleozoic and Mesozoic seas sweeping intermittently across Wyoming, the waters finally withdrew 85 million years ago, leaving a horizontal sedimentary blanket several scores of miles thick. Over 30,000 feet of Mesozoic rocks were deposited in western Wyoming, as well as eastern Wyoming's colorful Morrison shales that entombed some of the world's finest dinosaur bones.

Near the close of the Mesozoic era, the flat monotonous landscape was about to be changed dramatically, in one of the most exciting and important chapters in the geologic history of North America, the birth of the Rocky Mountains.

Left: Looking across the Precambrian rocks of Alaska Basin at the rumpled sedimentary layers of Paleozoic sea bottoms. Mt. Meek and its shelf tilts westward in the Jedediah Smith Wilderness, on the west flank of the Teton Range. LORRAINE G. BONNEY

Above: Brachiopod fossil hundreds of millions of years old lived in warm, shallow sea, before uplift of the Wind River Range where this was photographed. BILL RATCLIFFE

What tremendous force caused these upturned ridges of sedimentary slabs around Hoback Peak in the Wyoming Range to skid eastward 50 to 75 miles to "overthrust" other layers and pile up like overlapping shingles?
CHARLES FROIDERAUX

The Laramide Orogeny

The cause of the great mountain-building period of the Laramide Orogeny is very debatable. What struck the continent with enough force to kick off a 40-million-year orgy of intense folding, faulting and mountain-building in the western third of the continent? Whatever it was created a slow great wave that surged from the west into Wyoming. Its leading front of new-generation mountains deformed the land as they rose progressively eastward, lifting western Wyoming above sea level.

According to the National Geographic Society, about 65 million years ago the old, cold, heavy Pacific seafloor collided with the western edge of North America. The seafloor dove beneath the continent and the overriding continental plate was compressed near its margin. The converging plates, moving at the geologically breathtaking speed of 15 centimeters a year, triggered deepseated earthquakes, the effects prompted the *Laramide Orogeny*. Forty million years of earth-shaking mountain building uplifted the western landscape from the Sierra Nevada to the Rocky Mountains and Black Hills of Wyoming.

Did it all happen in Wyoming as plate tectonic theorists say—west-coast action reaching across the miles? Scientists currently disagree on applying plate tectonic theory to Wyoming landforms.

With no colliding continents handy, what hit the continent with enough force to drive the Overthrust Belt Mountains some 50 to 75 miles east and what kicked off the rise of the foreland mountains? (These steeply uplifted compressional mountain ranges of central and eastern Wyoming had been on the "foreland" of the continental margins at the time of their mountain origins.) One very notable tectonic coincidence at the time of the Laramide Orogeny, notes John McPhee in his book *Rising from the Plains*— on geologist Dr. Dave Love—was the opening of the Atlantic Ocean in mid-Mesozoic times. North America slid west, abutting the Pacific Plate, something like a great rug sliding across a room to crumple up in wrinkles against the far wall. But then again, that was way over there, not here.

Dave Love says that, since the Rockies are a thousand miles from the nearest plate boundary, we shouldn't tie in the landscape here with events along the coast. McPhee quotes Love: "This doesn't neutralize or dispose of the theory of plate tectonics, but applied here it's incongruous...There is no evidence of plates grinding against each other here. The thrust sheets are probably symptoms of plate-tectonic activity 50 million years ago, but the chief problem is that tectonism is not adequately placed in a time framework here ... Until we know the anatomy of each mountain range, how are we going to say what came up when—or if they all came up in one great spasm."

The Rocky Mountains Are Born

Mountain-making crustal movements had first begun rumbling in Utah and Idaho in mid-Mesozoic time. As the Mesozoic closed, the Rockies began to rise—the Wind River, Granite and Medicine Bow ranges uplifting into broad gentle "French loaf" arches as they staked out their ancestral sites. The first crustal movement in the Teton area in latest Cretaceous time developed a broad, low north-trending arch, ancestor of the Teton-Gros Ventre ranges. As the older ranges continued to rise, the Beartooth and Owl Creek ranges, the western part of the Gros Ventre Range, the Washakie Range and Black Hills started rising.

By early Cenozoic time all the major mountain ranges in Wyoming were outlined, except the north-trending part of the Teton Range, the Absaroka Range, and the eastern half of the Gros Ventre Range. All the major basins were formed. For unknown reasons, the dinosaurs were losing their battle for survival; the "Golden Age of Mammals" was about to begin.

The Rise and Fall of Mountain Empires

The shortest, most exciting and violent era of all, the Cenozoic, a mere 65 million years, is the final half inch on the geologic yardstick. It is the time when the Laramide Orogeny geared into full swing. Again, according to the National Geographic Society, internal heat, seeking to escape, set continents and ocean floors in motion. The resulting earthquakes and volcanism broke the crust into a patchwork of rigid plates that rode on the churning, viscous mantle below. Grinding past each other in fits and starts, the plates left great rips, or faults, in their journey. Strain built up along "locked" plate edges until something had to give; the stress could be released gradually by thousands of tiny earthquakes, or unleashed in a single disastrous jolt.

When that happened, as a likely effect, the surface of Wyoming became rumpled by powerful underground compressive forces, finally culminating in the building of most of Wyoming's major mountain ranges. Large-scale crustal movements tilted and fractured, twisted, warped and faulted the once neatly layered sedimentary rocks of the old seabeds. Some basins downwarped 30,000' or more and some mountains upwarped at least 14,000'. Great thrust faults shook Wyoming's southwest quarter. When this astonishing movement of mountain blocks was over, "rootless" remnant sedimentary top-layers from Utah and perhaps Idaho—had been skidded east some 50 to 75 miles over younger rocks into eastern Idaho and

southwest Wyoming. They piled up like overlapping shingles against the rooted Gros Ventre and ancestral Teton ranges in Jackson Hole, forming the Wyoming segment of the now-famous Overthrust Belt. Movement ranged from tens of miles in the Overthrust Belt directly south of the Tetons to fewer than five miles on the east margin of Jackson Hole (the west flank of the Washakie Range). The earth's crust bowed up gradually to form a broad arch that was the framework of the ancestral Teton-Gros Ventre uplift. Miles below, along the Buck Mountain fault, a large mass of rock was uplifted more than a thousand feet, modifying the framework of the original Teton block in a significant way, and setting the stage for the erosional effects resulting from future uplift of the Tetons.

In contrast to the Overthrust Belt, a tectonic event occurred in the foreland mountains (those east of the thrust

The Wind River Range punched through a 20,000' sedimentary crust. Like giant mushrooms, the peaks burst through the earth in a blink of geologic time. This is Camel's Hump from the South Fork of the Wind River. GEORGE WUERTHNER

7

Right: Looking like giant waves of a sea swell, these timber-covered seabottom sedimentaries of the Gros Ventre uplift are a topsy-turvy seascape gone wild. In contrast to the faulted Tetons with no foothills, the Gros Ventres are folded mountains with foothills. GEORGE WUERTHNER

WYOMING'S GEOLOGICAL TIME LINE

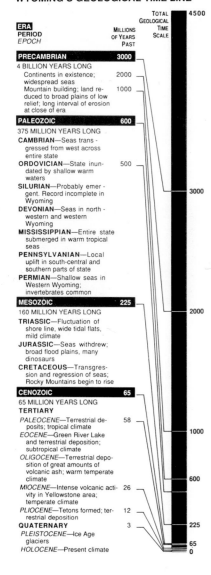

ERA PERIOD *EPOCH*	MILLIONS OF YEARS PAST	TOTAL GEOLOGICAL TIME SCALE
		4500
PRECAMBRIAN	**3000**	
4 BILLION YEARS LONG		
Continents in existence; widespread seas	2000	
Mountain building; land reduced to broad plains of low relief; long interval of erosion at close of era	1000	
PALEOZOIC	**600**	
375 MILLION YEARS LONG		
CAMBRIAN—Seas transgressed from west across entire state		
ORDOVICIAN—State inundated by shallow warm waters	500	3000
SILURIAN—Probably emergent. Record incomplete in Wyoming		
DEVONIAN—Seas in northwestern and western Wyoming		
MISSISSIPPIAN—Entire state submerged in warm tropical seas		
PENNSYLVANIAN—Local uplift in south-central and southern parts of state		
PERMIAN—Shallow seas in Western Wyoming; invertebrates common		
MESOZOIC	**225**	
160 MILLION YEARS LONG		2000
TRIASSIC—Fluctuation of shore line, wide tidal flats, mild climate		
JURASSIC—Seas withdrew; broad flood plains, many dinosaurs		
CRETACEOUS—Transgression and regression of seas; Rocky Mountains begin to rise		
CENOZOIC	**65**	
65 MILLION YEARS LONG **TERTIARY**		
PALEOCENE—Terrestrial deposits; tropical climate	58	
EOCENE—Green River Lake and terrestrial deposition; subtropical climate		1000
OLIGOCENE—Terrestrial deposition of great amounts of volcanic ash; warm temperate climate		
MIOCENE—Intense volcanic activity in Yellowstone area; temperate climate	26	600
PLIOCENE—Tetons formed; terrestrial deposition	12	
QUATERNARY	3	225
PLEISTOCENE—Ice Age glaciers		65
HOLOCENE—Present climate		0

belt) that would be unique to the western hemisphere. Over a span of time, starting with the Wind River Range and ending with the Laramie Range, these restless mountains punched their way through a 20,000' cover of sedimentary crust, shattering it and then, like Atlas, shrugging the debris off. The erosion of tilted sedimentary layers produced landforms called "hogbacks" along the margins of the ranges. The sedimentary debris itself was transported into and completely filled the basins adjacent to the uplifting ranges. A huge wedge of the crust was pushed toward the southwest to form the Wind River

Range, eventually standing thousands of feet above the surrounding topography.

Geologists are perplexed over what caused this massive mountain-building event. The Winds lurched southwest some five inches in every 10 years, for a million years, and part of the Bighorns inched south, the other east. The Beartooths headed east and southwest. The Medicine Bows moved east, the Washakie Range west, the Sierra Madre stayed put. Unlike the Overthrust Belt, in which rock sheets were moved laterally long distances and detached

8

from their roots, the mountain ranges of central and eastern Wyoming were moved along more steeply dipping faults while remaining attached to their basal roots.

These mountains were not in neat parallel lines as were those in the Overthrust Belt. Like a dropped armload of firewood, the spines of the ranges faced around in unconforming trends—the Winds and Bighorns pointing northwest-southeast; the Laramie Range north-south; the Owl Creeks lined up east to west, the Washakie Range half and half.

At any rate, when the Laramide Orogeny climaxed 50 to 55 million years ago, its chore of building Wyoming's major structural features—the mountains and basins, as we see them today—had been accomplished. Exceptions were the eastern Gros Ventre Range, the Tetons and the Absaroka Range.

Even as the mountains rose, they became the battlefield of the forces that raise mountains and the slow, relentless processes of erosion striving to level them. Erosion would win, eroding the mountain cores and filling adjacent basins, thus burying the relief that once characterized those basins, recreating the featureless plain that once had been. Then a new form of violence erupted to change the geological picture.

Volcanoes

A completely different type of earth history began in the early Eocene, a period of intense volcanic activity from today's Montana south to Texas. A thousand vents in northwestern Wyoming poured out lava by the cubic mile, first in the southern Absaroka Range, then from the central Absarokas and Yellowstone area, and smaller volcanic vents in the Rattlesnake Hills and Black Hills areas. Soon the Washakie and Owl Creek Mountains were buried so deep that the Wind River and Bighorn basins fused above them.

And still the volcanic area grew in size, violence and volume of debris until Pliocene time. Burning through the earth's crust like blasts from a flamethrower, magma flooded to the surface to build massive volcanoes. Tremendous volumes of debris belched forth from the central Absaroka Range and northwest corner of Yellowstone Park, spreading several thousand feet thick across eastern Jackson Hole. Powerful streams carried away the coarse debris. Ash was carried by wind for hundreds of miles,

covering all of Wyoming, arcing into Montana, the Dakotas, Nebraska and Colorado, filling the basins and drowning the earlier topography. The process took only 20 million years. So much airborne volcanic debris choked up the streams that they lost their erosive powers.

By late Miocene, only the upper 1,000 to 4,000 feet of the highest peaks in Wyoming's major mountain ranges poked above the featureless alluvial plain. Wind River summits were just a small range of hills. From them a few sluggish streams meandered into the Gulf of Mexico.

And still the Yellowstone-Absaroka volcanoes and a new hot spot, the northwest side of the Teton region, blasted on. This outpouring would directly affect the subsidence of Jackson Hole and the rise of the Tetons.

The volcanic origin of Wyoming's northwest is revealed in the rhyolite outcrops of Bunsen Peak, Yellowstone National Park. It is the eroded remnant of a volcanic neck.
KENT & DONNA DANNEN

WEST TO EAST STRUCTURAL CROSS-SECTION OF WYOMING

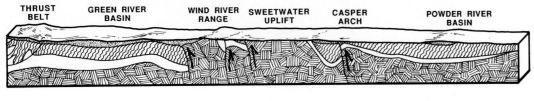

THRUST BELT　　GREEN RIVER BASIN　　WIND RIVER RANGE　SWEETWATER UPLIFT　　CASPER ARCH　　POWDER RIVER BASIN

▨ PRECAMBRIAN　☐ PALEOZOIC　▨ MESOZOIC　▨ TERTIARY

Left: Schoolbook Glacier, in the Teton Range, is small enough to show many features of glacial action in a small area. RON MAMOT

Right: The glaciated U-shaped valley of North Fork Cascade Canyon showing Mt. Owen and the Three Tetons to the west. PAT O'HARA

Diagram: Cross sections showing development of geologic structure across Wyoming. COURTESY OF THE GEOLOGICAL SURVEY OF WYOMING

By late Tertiary the Gros Ventre Range had been completed. Its overriding block had been thrust southwest against the northern end of the Overthrust ranges. The ancestral Teton Range, contemporary extension of the ancestral Gros Ventres, was still the low series of hills produced by the Buck Mountain Fault during the Laramide Orogeny. Then the Teton landscape ruptured along the 50-mile Teton fault. West of the fault the Tetons began to rise rapidly. East of the fault the land sank, creating Jackson Hole. The total displacement between the two blocks was some 24,000 feet.

As floods leave highwater marks, so, too, the volcanic era left its high-level mark on Wyoming mountains between 11,000' and 12,000' above sea level, mute testimony to the maximum limit of mountain burial during late Tertiary time.

Because of three factors—the end of volcanic activity, something called an epierogeny, and the climatic accident of the Pleistocene Ice Age—western Wyoming especially was about to undergo a tremendous face lift.

Born Again! Exhumation of the Rockies

As the Tertiary closed, an epierogeny, a broad and general continental uplift, quickly raised Wyoming to its present mile-high elevation above sea level, and boosted the mountain tops to their 12,000'-13,000' levels.

As the Tertiary gave way to the Quaternary period, the streams wandering sluggishly and aimlessly over the Miocene plain and overloaded with volcanic debris, responded to the continental uplift. They straightened out, quickened, began to cut and erode, pushing around boulders and gravels and cutting channels. The revitalized late Tertiary river systems superimposed across the buried mountain ranges needed only 3 million years to strip off the entire Tertiary cover, a matter of getting rid of some 50,000 cubic miles of rock from around and over Wyoming ranges alone. Basins were re-excavated, buried mountain ranges exhumed. New faces were cut in the older rocks, exposing the resistant Precambrian mountain cores.

And the streams? Their channels bore no relationship to the Eocene topography buried far below. Industriously they cut their way down through the Miocene blanket. If they happened on to a buried mountain range, they sawed right through the ridge. Irrespective of modern topography, the river patterns are Miocene.

Take Wind River, for instance. It, with its tributaries, heads in the Wind River Range and southern Absarokas, flowing mostly east and then northeast through Wind River Basin to collide with the Owl Creek Mountains near Thermopolis. Did it detour? Not at all. It just cut its Wind River Canyon through the range and came out below as the Bighorn River. It fooled the early explorers, who thought it was two rivers heading in the same range, until the canyon was discovered.

The North Platte River and its several main branches are another anomaly. The North Platte heads in Colorado south of Mountain Home, Wyoming, flows north through the rocks of the Medicine Bows, crosses Hanna Basin, then cuts through the Seminoe and Granite mountains where it is joined by the Sweetwater River on the crest of the Granite Mountains Uplift. The Sweetwater, coming out of the southern Winds, flowed across a flat surface of sedimentary fill that once covered the Granite Mountains, eventually being "let down" into the resistant granitic rocks. Trapped, it formed the Devils Gate, a short anomalous canyon.

The Laramie River started out conventionally enough, flowing northeast out of the southern end of the Medicine Bow Range (sometimes called the Rawah Range), and north along the west side of the Laramie Range. Then it turns hard right eastward across this major range as if the mountains didn't exist, its wild waters rushing through the deep rugged canyon of its own making.

The Quaternary Period, time of preglacial lakes, more crustal disturbances, and at least three glacial episodes, takes up less than 15 thousandths of the last inch on the geologic yardstick of time, with the entire Ice Age taking up less than 2 thousandths of an inch, yet the effects

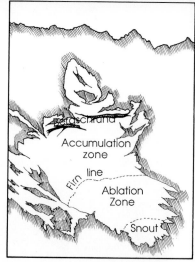

Left: Rock surface polished and deeply grooved by glacier.
GRAND TETON NATIONAL PARK
Above: Anatomy of a glacier.
LAUREL BLACK, ANAGLYPH ART SERVICES

of nature's Quaternary forces on the northwest corner of Wyoming have been spectacular.

Northwestern Wyoming escaped the continental ice sheets of the Pleistocene epoch. It was, however, a part of the largest of 75 separate glaciated areas south of the continental ice cap in the western United States. This largest of ice-covered areas included part of Yellowstone Park, the Teton, Absaroka, Beartooth, Wind River and Gros Ventre ranges. Large piedmont ice masses, in places several thousand feet thick, accumulated in northwestern Wyoming, and smaller glaciers developed in the Bighorn, Medicine Bow and Sierra Madre ranges.

At least three times (four in the Wind River Range) in the last 250,000 years, rivers of ice from the Beartooth–Yellowstone–Absaroka ice center scraped their way past the Tetons through Jackson Hole, a great meeting ground of ice. The Teton, Gros Ventre and Wind River ranges supplied lesser amounts of ice.

Humans appeared during the last one fiftieth of an inch on our yardstick of time gone by. In this short span they have had more impact on the earth and its inhabitants than any other form of life.

VEGETATION

Mountain ash. GEORGE WUERTHNER

Right: The colorful meadows of Cliff Creek's subalpine zone in the Wyoming Range. This is game range—grassy parks, aspen groves, sage slopes, pine and fir forests. The Gros Ventre Range is on the skyline. GEORGE WUERTHNER

Wyoming's vegetation is one of its wonders, as varied as its landscape, ranging from desert to arctic plants, from the common to the rare and strange; with an ability to support record populations from fish to elk and big-horns; able to support the nutritional and medicinal needs of nomadic Indians as they followed the harvest cycle right into the mountains; with a diversity of plants that, like an almanac, can tell a person when elk calves are being born, when Canada geese eggs are hatching, or, for the fisherman, when salmon flies are hovering over the streams.

A visitor driving along U.S. Highway 89-191 in Jackson Hole looks across the Snake River valley to the Tetons and sees cottonwoods in the floodplains, lodgepole pine and sagebrush flats on the benches, and fringing the lower Teton slopes are pines and firs dotted with aspen groves. This casual view is taking in the five major plant commu-nities of Wyoming mountains—sagebrush-grass, lodge-pole pine (ponderosa pine in the drier east), Douglas fir, spruce-fir, and alpine.

The hiker climbing a mountain can savor all the zones from grasses to arctic tundra because they are all compressed here, accordion-like, within a mile of elevation. It is the equivalent of a several-thousand-mile trip north through deciduous and coniferous forest zones up to arctic tundra. The common denominator, of course, is the cold. It gets colder as one goes north where the sun's rays tilt more and more, just as it gets colder as one goes up a mountain, because the thinner air holds less heat. The hiker gets first-hand knowledge of the geology and the animals, and the vegetative changes that can tell him how high he is and the basic type of rock he's on. As he climbs he follows the "Bloom Belt"—long after his favorite flowers have faded in the valley, the dwarf versions are blooming in the alpine tundra.

Left: Yucca at sunrise on the east slope of the Bighorn Mountains. The rain clouds have dropped their loads before reaching eastern Wyoming. Replacing the thirstier lodgepole pines of western Wyoming, the ponderosa thrives here, as do desert cacti. GEORGE WUERTHNER

Above: Parry primrose clings tena-ciously for existence in the rocky environment of the Tetons. PAT O'HARA

13

A hiker knows he's getting high when he enters the whitebark pine forest as here in the Teton Range. The whitebark, very windfirm, needs some 250 years to reach maturity. Found only in the northwest corner of Wyoming, its terrain extends northwards.
PAT O'HARA

The climbing hiker gets a fine overview of the sagebrush flats and lodgepole pine ridges of the rocky valley floor, the glittering lakes encircled by moraine dams. Pushing upwards, the climber sees that the mountainside belongs to the fir and pine, with each zone having its dominant conifers. Douglas firs continue to about 8,000', in elevation, mainly on the sunny sides of the canyons. Elk and mule deer, squirrels and marmots and all sorts of birds—grouse, flickers, juncos, woodpeckers, nuthatches, sparrows—like the big shady trees that can become 400 to 600 years of age and four to five feet in diameter.

A considerable portion of Wyoming mountain slopes lies within the subalpine life zone, up to timberline. The dark, spiky-needled Engelmann spruce with its hanging cones and its companion, the soft-needled fir with upright cones thrive on the cold, wet, north-facing slopes. The moose loves it here winter or summer be-cause its favorite winter food, the subalpine fir, is on the increase throughout this zone. Many other animals and birds live here in summer—elk, mule deer, Uinta ground squirrels, pine martens, porcupines, weasels, mountains lions, the occasional passing wolverine, blue grouse, woodpeckers and owls, flycatchers and jays. The switch-backing trail crosses foaming creeks porcelained with silt from the glaciers above, veers toward a thundering cas-cade where its erosive powers work at wearing down the "eternal hills."

Near timberline the views open up. Talus slopes, avalanche slides and boulder fields increase. The evergreens thin out, dwindle into stunted timberline trees—gnarled, windbeaten whitebark pine, scraggles of ground-hugging krummholz. Elfin timber, wind-bent and dense, hunkered in the shelter of protective objects, krummholz growth becomes more prostrate, more gnarled and contorted, with altitude. The eccentric topiary shapes mark the knife-edge boundary between a favorable microclimate and one of colder temperatures and abrasive, drying winds.

This is timberline, controlled by summer temperature, beyond which trees cannot survive. This is the edge of the alpine tundra—land of boulder fields, talus and scree slopes, stone or fellfields, and alpine meadows, mostly herbacous plants along with a few dwarf shrubs existing in a very cool and frequently moist climate on scanty soil. Their rock-strewn surfaces support a cover of grasses and sedges that provides summer forage for pika, elk and bighorn sheep.

To the hiker this is the landscape of ultimate freedom, among the high gliders, wind battered ridges, and the humbling "belly" plants, a breathless place, where rapid movement is an effort. Few things stay here in winter but summer finds golden eagles and ravens soaring on the air currents, horned larks, white-crowned sparrows, black-rosy finches, water pipits, and Clark's nutcracker. The sun-loving yellow-bellied marmot, the busy little Uinta chipmunk, golden-mantled ground squirrels and pikas add to the fascination of alpine country.

This is special country, rarefied yet exhilarating atmos-phere, this intense land of contrasts—the cold, windy, challenging world of rock, versus the tough world of dauntless microscopic mosaics, where the sky is forever and the flowers the size of a millisecond.

14

Alpine tundra is gently rolling land, rock-littered, surrounded by peaks and cliffs, breezy, soaked by snowmelt and high altitude rains. It sports ankle-deep carpets of velvety grasses, sedges and flowers like storybook meadows—green cushions sequined with water drops, gurgling streamlets winding around miniature elfin gardens. Above the tundra the tiny pioneer plants cling precariously to rock crevices and ledges; lichens stain the rock, a few hardy species that are the truly alpine and arctic element of mountain flora, where the process of primary succession works.

Here the eagle-eyed hiker could discover the ultimate botanical trinity near his boots—three brilliant dwarf alpine flowers that embody the beauty of the mountain flora. The velvet green cushion of moss campion

smothered with tiny pink flowers may grow side by side with the bright blues of the forget-me-not and the white phlox to create a cushioned mosaic of red, white and blue. They are the scenic climax of mountain vegetation, the jackpot of tundra glories. When the moss pink is in full bloom the water pipit, white-crowned sparrow and the gray-crowned rosy finch are laying their eggs.

Through studying prehistoric ecology (paleoecology) we catch glimpses of climate and vegetation changes spanning millions of years, although volcanic activity and glaciation have greatly obscured the record. The best fossils came from the Eocene epoch, which had a subtropical Gulf Coast climate with palm trees and deciduous forests.

Left: Moss campion. JEFF FOOTT *Top: White phlox.* JOHN J. SMITH *Center: Alpine forget-me-nots.* BILL RATCLIFFE *Bottom: Krummholz, or elfin wood.* JEFF FOOTT

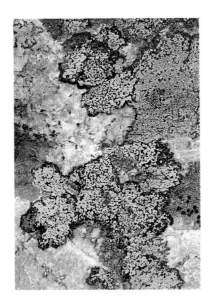

Above: Lichens are specialized plants consisting of algae and fungi. They grow extremely slowly and persist for years.
Right: The lodgepole pine is king in Yellowstone National Park. The Absaroka Range is on the horizon.
PAT O'HARA PHOTOS

The Pleistocene ice masses scoured much of the land down to bedrock, destroying all plant life in their advance, but a circumpolar reservoir of plants escaped either by spreading ahead of the glaciers or by remaining stranded on isolated unglaciated peaks or ridges. Soon after the glaciers retreated, alpine tundra took over, followed by subalpine meadows with spruce, fir and whitebark pine. As warmer climates and better soils developed, the pioneers were slowly replaced by a diversity of other vegetation as plants moved in from the south, following the receding ice-front and eventually reoccupying all the land once covered by ice. The glaciers spread moss campion throughout the world's high country, from the Scottish highlands, the peaks of the Alps and tundras of the north, to the high Rockies. It has taken moss campion clumps centuries to reach present size. Other plants found at this elevation are grass, alpine phlox, dryad, dwarf clover, nailwort, arctic gentian, rose crown, sedge, goldenrod, yellow stone-crop, sandwort, grass, fairy primrose, willow, dwarf willow, currant, bistort, alpine forget-me-not, shrubby cinquefoil, star gentian.

In the sparse mountain soils, the simplest plant form, crustose-lichen, prepares the bare rock for the foliose-lichen stage to take over on the meager substratum. Gradually the rock, sand or soil is altered and conditioned, made optimum, by each lower plant stage for the next more complex level to move in. Mosses give way to herabaceous plants, then shrubs to subclimax forests, to the final climax forest—the ultimate use of an area.

Ecological succession ends with the development of stable, self-perpetuating and complex climax communities. Major events—fire, insect epidemics, logging, grazing, land- and snowslides, windstorms—can disturb them, but seemingly small things can also change, even make or break, a community. The dominant or climax plant, able to reproduce itself and prevent other plants from taking over, remains king because it has fine-tuned itself to conditions—elevation, direction and steepness of slope, climate, wind patterns, shade tolerance, water and soil needs. The replacement of one plant community by another usually follows an orderly, predictable pattern—called succession—where progressive changes tip the balance in favor of other dominant species.

Fire played a major role in shaping the forests of Wyo-

ming's mountain ranges, and fire suppression has played an equally important part in changing those communities.

Wildfires once occurred often, usually as small, creeping ground fires that could persist for months, burning out ground litter and leaving little organic trash to feed larger fires. Large, intense and widespread fires were rare but when they occurred their effects were significant. Fire scars have been traced as far back as the 1600s. Because of recurring fires throughout Wyoming's forested areas, large tracts of merchantable-sized timber were scarce in the last century.

Half a century of fire suppression changed all that, as the protected, dominant lodgepole forests matured and spread extensively, aspen groves declined and big sage-brush replaced herbaceous communities. As fire–resistant communities were eliminated, a more uniform eco-system developed, putting ecological succession toward climax communities on hold. This in turn cut down on the number of types of wildlife habitat, and hence types of wildlife.

A good example of the effects of fire suppression can be seen in the northwest corner of Wyoming. Here the lodgepole pine is continuous in almost pure stands from the Absaroka Range foothills, across the Yellowstone plateau and rolling hills of the Bridger-Teton National Forest down to the south flank of the Teton Range. When the climate warmed after the glaciers retreated, the lodge-poles came in some 11,500 years ago and have persisted ever since. They regenerated very well after fires, seed-lings producing a very dense, even-aged stand often bare of understory plants, soil layers and birds. Fire suppression has allowed this tree to reach ages of 80 to 100 years, the age when they are most susceptible to mountain pine beetles.

Without fires, the pine beetle has become epidemic throughout the west. As the even-aged lodgepole forests reach 80 to 100 years of age, beetle populations explode. They turn great patches of the rich dark-green mantle into burnished brown, then lifeless gray, acres. Wyoming winds knock over the shallow-rooted dead timber into a downed web of combustible matchsticks, ready for a spark. Today the National Park Service and the Forest Service are allowing some naturally-caused fires in the back country to burn themselves out.

Top: This even-age stand of matchstick lodgepole pine has thinned itself out. D. CAVAGNARO
Bottom: Old burn near Deer Lake in the Bighorns. THOMAS BEAN

WILDLIFE

The kingly bald eagle is a thrilling sight. It is very much on the endangered list, especially in Jackson Hole. Dam construction and overuse of the oxbow and of the Snake River at the wrong times have contributed to poor reproduction. DENNIS M. HENRY

The Shoshones called the ungainly moose the "black elk." It was the final big animal made by Father Above, who combined the unused and left-over parts still around. JEFF FOOTT

The "Golden Age of Mammals" began with the Cretaceous extinction of the great dinosaurs. Since that time a strange and motley assortment of creatures has paraded in and out of the Wyoming scene as its climates and landscapes shifted into the Tertiary Period of tropical to temperate climates, the Laramide Orogeny and volcanic outbursts, then moved into the Ice Age, and on to the present.

During the early Tertiary time of intense volcanic activity in northwestern Wyoming 40 to 50 million years ago, the state had a gulf coast climate, deciduous forests, with southern garden red roses, climbing ferns, hibiscus, goldenrain. Eocene lakes had 12-foot crocodiles, 40-pound gars, catfish, stingrays, herring and trout perch, among others, later—20 to 30 million years ago in Oligocene and Miocene time. For the first time in geologic history grasslands became prominent enough to support a great variety of animals. Besides rhinoceroses, camels, peccaries, saber-toothed cats and mastodons, the first of Wyoming's big game types—the prongbuck "antelope"— appeared with wide variation in horn types, several types of horses including three-toed ones were numerous; and large wolf-like dogs, burrowing beavers, squirrel-like rodents and rabbits were about.

Four million years ago the volcanic activity diminished and the Tetons were raised to their present height. Eighty percent of the families of terrestrial mammals then present are still around in modern forms. Rhinos became rare but prongbucks, camels and horses flourished. Carnivores were abundant and primitive bears appeared for the first time as bear-like dogs and short-faced dogs.

The Ice Age in general was characterized by extreme climatic conditions, shifting from arctic to warm, even arid climates between ice advances. The ancestors of the bighorn crossed to North America from Asia during the ice ages and spread downwards. Common fossils of the ice ages include horses, mastodons, mammoths, camels and bison. Less common were prongbuck, peccary, rodents and carnivores.

Within a few thousand years after the ice age, camels, horses, mastodons, mammoths and ground sloths were extinct in North America. Why? They vanished from an environment to which they were well adapted; horses and camels survived in Europe and Africa in similar environ-

Left: Wild stallions fighting at a water hole in the Continental Divide Basin.
Below: A welcome dust bath for the monarch of the plains.
JEFF FOOTT PHOTOS

Above:The pronghorn antelope, lightest and speediest of the big-game animals, has remarkable eyesight. The remains of its ancestors of 20,000 years ago have been found in Wyoming. JEFF FOOTT

Right: The mule deer, whose hearing is especially good because of its mule-like ears, was first called "muley" by the early white hunters.
DENNIS M. HENRY

ments. Most of these animals had been in existence when humans arrived in North America. The oldest record of humans in Wyoming is 11,000 years ago and we know he hunted these beasts. Some scientists believe that early man was responsible for their extinction. But the mystery of the Pleistocene extinctions remains to be solved.

Since the ice ages, 6,000 to 8,000 years ago, North American animals have remained about the same except that modern man has greatly reduced their numbers and changed their environment in the last 150 years.

Wyoming has been a prime hunting ground since the ice ages. The Indians fought for these grounds—among themselves and against the white man. The fur trapper found the country rich in pelts. However, Wyoming's golden age of hunting went out with the fur trappers, the

hide hunters, elk tuskers, the 19th-century sportsmen of Europe like Sir St. George Gore who massacred 2,000 buffalo, 100 bears, 1,600 elk and deer, just for sport, on a three-year hunting trip, 1854-1857.

As the West was settled, problems began for the animals—they had to compete with livestock, endure new diseases, survive the hunters. Populations of many— beaver, bison, moose and deer—were drastically reduced. The elk, grizzly and coyote backed off from the prairies and valleys, taking to the rugged terrain of the mountains.

Here, the vertical compression of ecological zones on mountains came to the rescue of the retreating animals. Because, on a mountain slope, a wide variety of habitat and food resources exists within a short distance, animals could take advantage of this accordion-like squeeze. In

the closely packed but sharply contrasting life zones, when the weather turns severe, alpine residents like the bighorn sheep move from tundra to timberline for protection and food.

Bighorn sheep and mountain goats thrive on high rugged terrain where cold is the enemy, footing is precarious, vegetation is limited and shelter is scarce. Some of the smaller mammals burrow or hibernate to beat the cold. Other alpine animals develop extra-heavy coats, such as the mountain goat—a relative newcomer to Wyoming mountains after successful transplants.

This century has seen the establishment of wilderness areas and enlightened game management that have assured the future of prized big-game animals by transplanting, planned hunting, refuges and artificial feeding.

Far left top: Trumpeter swan, a favorite sighting for Yellowstone and Grand Teton park visitors. JEFF FOOTT
Far left bottom: Goshawk with young. JEFF FOOTT

Near left: It's a rare treat to catch a glimpse of a cougar or mountain lion. Remains of their ancestors have been found in the Bighorns' Natural Trap Cave. JESS R. LEE

Above: Another rare sight is the pine marten, whose ancestors were in Wyoming more than 20,000 years ago. ERWIN & PEGGY BAUER

Top: The pika, above-timberline denizen identified by his shrill whistle and "haystacks" drying for winter. JEFF FOOTT

Bottom: The black rosy finch and its cousins brown and gray rosy finches are welcome sights high in the mountains. JEFF FOOTT

Right: An old ram (horn dominance is a special feature of bighorn sheep society), guarding his ewes, barks a warning to young intruders. RON MAMOT

Rocky Mountain Bighorn Sheep

As a true wilderness species, the Rocky Mountain bighorn sheep *(Ovis canadensis)* requires wilderness for its existence, habitat with highly specific vegetational and topographic characteristic; areas that man has disturbed very little or not at all.

Such a place is the Whiskey Mountain natural winter range in the Wind River Range, which caters to the tough requirements of the largest single herd of bighorn sheep in the world.

Between 800 and 1,000 head of this relatively scarce species thrive on thousands of acres of steep grassy sidehills separated by sheer-sided canyons thousands of feet deep. Unique climatic-geologic conditions save the area from heavy snowfall. Any snow is blown into drifts by the incessant Wyoming wind, exposing the nutritious wild grasses.

Bighorns have been wintering at Whiskey Mountain probably since the end of the ice ages. The ancient "sheepeater" Indians survived on the bighorns—getting from them meat, clothes and utensils. In 1952 only 250 sheep were left of the once-large herds and restoration steps were taken.

Bighorns are naturally devastated by winter hardships after being greatly stressed by the rutting season. In early November the summer-fattened animals descend to the wintering grounds. By late November the rut is in full swing, with rams squaring off in classic battles to establish a pecking order. For a chaotic month and a half the mountain is alive with running rams, some chasing, others fleeing, but all running. Rams chase estrous ewes and smaller rams, knock heads with same-size rams, and get knocked about by larger rams. The ewes in heat have to be chased and chased into exhaustive submission throughout their two-day estrous period. By the end of the rut all the bighorns, rams and ewes, are worn out and in very weakened condition. During winter they become extremely lethargic, conserving their energy to survive the winter. Seclusion is important. Any harassment consumes critical reserves, so an established, protected winter range is an absolute necessity.

Yellowstone Grizzly

The great bear of the West, the grizzly *(Ursus arctos horribilis)* is not necessarily a predator. He likes a steady diet of ground squirrels, grass, berries and roots, but will never pass up a mired elk or moose. He demands solitude, a square meal and 270 kilometers of home range.

So what's his problem as his numbers decline in the vast fount of wilderness in and around Yellowstone National Park, which has been his home for centuries? Bears, grizzly and black alike, are scavengers and gorgers. Lewis and Clark, poling up the Missouri in 1805, found the bears stuffing themselves on dead buffalo— killed by drowning or by Indians at buffalo jumps—or gorging at spawning sites or on winter-killed elk. When civilization took over the rivers and plains, the bears moved onto the Yellowstone plateau and survived on winter-killed or rut-weakened elk from the huge herds there. After the Park was created, they gorged at garbage dumps.

24

In 1968, the Department of the Interior decided to return the natural areas of Yellowstone to their former primitive, self-regulating ecosystems—including closing all the garbage dumps by 1971. The dump-closure decision had been made because, as park visitations rose to the 2 million mark, so did the encounters between bears and visitors; also rising were claims against the National Park Service. Black bears did the most damage but the few grizzly bear incidents got the headlines because, unlike black bears, grizzlies occasionally kill people.

Biologists Frank and John Craighead, first to study the grizzly in the Park, had suggested a controlled, gradual closing of the dumps, with studies monitoring the effect on the bears, and supplemental feeding during the transition period. Thus began a bear-management controversy that rages today. Wildlife managers and researchers still are not in agreement as to whether the dump closures were a good or a bad thing, whether grizzly populations, which have declined in recent decades, are a result of the park's management policy or may be attributable to many other environmental factors, or for that matter exactly how many bears the park itself can sustain in a natural condition and whether that number is below the minimum population required for the grizzly to survive.

As a result of the controversy it is possible that the grizzly bear may have become the most studied wildlife species in U.S. history, but in spite of the studies, the question remains: Can the park sustain a naturally regulated population of grizzlies?

Probably the only thing almost everone who is concerned about the bear's continued existence can agree upon is that the bear needs more habitat than just Yellowstone Park, and habitat in and around the park is fast disappearing (e.g., Grant Village was built in an area that affected prime grizzly fishing streams). Natural causes created shortages in grizzly food—the spreading pine bark beetle was threatening the white bark pine, whose nut is the main food for grizzlies in the fall; overgrazing by a large elk population reduced the berry bushes and changed needed willow/aspen habitats for the bear.

This immense, omnivorous, space-loving animal requires an immense habitat in relationship to its minimum viable population. Unfortunately that habitat

Grizzly bear. JESS R. LEE

crosses a myriad of political jurisdictions—national parks, national and state forests, private property, county and state boundaries. With or without natural regulation of its population in the park, the bear already makes its home in that sprawl of Wyoming's wildlands known as the Greater Yellowstone ecosystem. Keeping its home intact may be the key to its survival.

Paleo man enjoyed the summer view of the 13,000' peaks of the Tetons for 6,000 years.
GEORGE WUERTHNER
Right: With the Jackson Lake dam under construction, the waters are now the lowest since 1915, allowing digs by National Park Service archaeologists and volunteers.
LORRAINE G. BONNEY

Teton Range. As it lifted in repeated sporadic jolts, the stratified sediments of a half a million years were carried upward on its tilted back and were shucked off westwards. Thus the two-generation, doubly uplifted Teton Range was born—its highest cluster wedged between the Teton Fault and the older Buck Mountain Fault!

At the same time east of the Teton fault, the floor of Jackson Hole, like another great trapdoor hinged in the eastern highlands, sank dramatically and rapidly along the fault at the base of the range. Its floor was sucked into the growing vacuum far below, replacing the semifluid rock or magma being pulled north into the erupting Yellowstone-Absaroka area. Abrasive waters scoured off the 20,000' of layered sediments from the blocky, shapeless Tetons, exposing the Precambrian core, but failed to remove some Cambrian sandstone from the highest summits, like that capping Mt. Moran. Its counterpart lay 30,000' lower—under the valley floor.

As the newborn Tetons were uplifted, they were simultaneously eroded, so that at any one time, the erosional and structural relief remained little more than what we see today, about 7,000' from valley floor to mountain summit.

Once the Tetons were lifted, new volcanoes in the Yellowstone hot spot inundated the north end with lava, rocks and flying ash. Then, 2 million years ago, more major faulting caused the valley block to drop even lower between the older Teton Fault and the newly formed Hoback Fault on the east side of the valley. About this time, also, a complex series of volcanic eruptions west and north of today's Jackson billowed forth various lavas and volcanic plugs, now called East and West Gros Ventre Buttes. The landscape began to look somewhat like that of today. Then the climate changed and the Ice Age moved in, about 200,000 or more years ago. During the first and most extensive Buffalo Glaciation, a thousand cubic miles of glacial river, half a mile thick, flowed from the Yellowstone, Beartooth and Absaroka ice centers. It bulldozed its way through the valley, overriding Signal Mountain and other mid-valley buttes as it scraped south along the Tetons, reaching above today's timberline. Another river of ice, spawned in the Wind River Range, flowed down the Gros Ventre River valley to merge with the main ice stream. They squeezed out of Jackson Hole by way of Snake River Canyon. When the Buffalo Glaciation was over, a devastated boulder field landscape was left behind.

The second—Bull Lake—glaciation, half as large, was followed by the Pinedale glaciation. The Pinedale, last and smallest is highly evident today. Its glaciers advanced down Cascade, Garnet, Avalanche and Death canyons, its ice dredging back into the mountains to cut cirques, sharpen the peaks and aretes. The glaciers spilled onto the floor of Jackson Hole, piling up moraines around the canyon mouths, then melted, leaving glittering piedmont lakes.

From the Gros Ventre Range, the eyes of Paleolithic man saw Jackson Hole still covered with the ice of Pinedale glaciers. They watched the glaciers shrink back into the mountains, retreating into shadowed crevices, then dwindle and die.

They watched as corrosive streams gnawed deeply through the range itself, forming a hydrographic divide one to three miles west of the original high Teton divide.

With the ice gone, these people of the high country camped every summer from about 9,000 years ago to 1600 A.D. in the huge camas meadows at the north end of the natural Jackson Lake, at a place now called the Lawrence site. They enjoyed the enormous hot springs at the base of the Tetons.

Because the diet of Paleo man centered on root crops, especially the blue camas (arrowhead and arrow leafed balsam root were others), these Native Americans utilized the Jackson Hole plant ecosystem for 6,000 years to a point just short of actual cultivation. During that time, the same base camps were continually revisited, the same raw materials, plants and animals were used as the two or three groups moved into the valley in late spring and into the high country (fall) exploiting its resources—fishing, gathering plants, hunting the scarce game. Serious winter hunting took place outside of Jackson Hole, probably in Idaho and southwestern Yellowstone. This was the pattern until around 1600 A.D. when something changed the status quo. The problem of hunting access reared its ugly head and brought an end to the only way of life that was completely in tune with the ecosystem of Jackson Hole.

By the 15th century, Shoshonean groups began migrating northeasterly out of the Great Basin, rapidly colonizing the semi-arid basins—the long-time winter hunting grounds of the high country people—thus cutting off access to hunting grounds. And the root eaters, with part of their resources (vital winter hunting grounds) lost to them, had to abandon the entire ecosystem, and so disappeared from the Jackson Hole scene.

Balsamroot, a staple of early man in Jackson Hole, blooms with the north end of the Teton Range in the background. GEORGE WUERTHNER

A closeup and an aerial view of Alaska Basin, Jedediah Smith Wilderness, Targhee National Forest.
PAT O'HARA PHOTOS

The Eastern Side

In 1906 and 1915 the U.S. Reclamation Service (now the U.S. Bureau of Reclamation) started building its large dam on Jackson Lake. The result was a dam sited on a small fault in a geologically active valley surrounded by major faults, only four miles from the Teton Fault, seven miles from the Spread Creek Fault, and 28 to 65 miles away from three other major fault zones.

In 1925, 75 million tons of rock slipped into the Gros Ventre River, triggered by earth tremors. Major earthquakes in 1959 and 1975 changed landforms and waterflow patterns. In 1983 the big spruces were discovered at the bottom of Jenny Lake, and an earthquake registering five on the Richter scale shook up the Hole.

In addition to the geological conflicts, political conflicts began raging when valley folks and outsiders realized what was here. Jackson Hole became the most controversial valley in the nation as this natural-born park area turned into a battleground; a horde of public and private interests struggled for its control like a pack of starving coyotes attacking a winter-weakened elk. Only two years were needed to take Yellowstone National Park from idea to fact, but it required 52 turbulent years to conclude the creation of a worthwhile Grand Teton National Park, finally achieved in 1950.

While many Jackson Holers feel their valley deserves a better future than as the supplier of 2x4's, beef for the table and water for Idaho spuds, they feel as though they're battling the devastating glaciers as they try to save their valley from powerful and destructive governmental forces and private interests. They must contend with an ever-expanding, controversial airport that is eating out the heart of Grand Teton Park.

They lost the battle of the precariously sited dam, being rebuilt, still in a hazardous fault area, at a cost of $82 million and four years of summer construction in the heart of the park. The simple answer was conservation! The historical needs of the Idaho farmers could have been met with Jackson Lake at its natural (non-dammed) level, if conservation methods (canal lining, etc.) were adopted at a cost of $102 million.

The Western Side

In sharp contrast to the east side of the Tetons with its exposures of tough Precambrian rock, the gentle western slope was neither fractured nor elevated as much and was shaped by all the debris—the 20,000' of layered sedimentaries and the broken hogbacks of Paleozoic and Mesozoic strata—that were draped around the Teton uplift, then stripped away by the elements.

On the west slope is the 116,535-acre Jedediah Smith Wilderness. Lying between the hydrographic divide and the Wyoming-Idaho border, its smooth slopes and rounded ridges were only lightly etched by glaciers. Streams here are less dynamic. The flat-topped mountains, resembling palisaded battlements of ancient fortresses, are the layered Paleozoic rocks of ancient seas. It contains glaciated basin lakes and ice-grooved floors in the snow-rock-grass mosaic of Alaska Basin— itself a geologic treasure of rock and fossil records of 120 million years. In its lower, shallow-sea sedimentaries exists a hoard of seabed fossil treasures—reefs like great stone anthills built by warm-water, blue-green algae now are found two miles above sea level, along with brachiopods, trilobites and stream-washed serpentine pebbles. Hikers seemingly float through deep, richly colored elysian meadows of softly blowing flowers, warm down-valley breezes at one's back, calm reflective lakes catching the images of stratified towers. Far from the crowds of the east-side park, solitude is one of the west side's treasures.

Some 53 caves, pits and holes, alpine karst phenomena, have been surveyed on the west side of the Tetons, clustered mostly at the south end, in the limestones from Rendezvous Peak to Darby Canyon. Among these caves are the impressive Wind Cave, the Darby Canyon Ice Cave, and Wyoming's deepest known vertical cave on Rendezvous Peak.

The wildest parts of the west-side Tetons are the north and south forks of Bitch Creek, which cut far back into the range at only about 6,000' to 7,000', in the montane zone of heavy timber and lush meadows. This stream provides some of the most exciting kayaking in the area.

The Wilderness Bill recognized that the entire north end of the Tetons was a critical link, for grizzlies, with Yellowstone Park. Nevertheless, the west side of this superb habitat is a wildlife vacuum except for a few bears and squirrels. Its problems stem from heavy sheep grazing and the fact that local users consider it their private backyard hunting ground year-round. It is probably the wettest place in Wyoming, with a 50-inch rainfall. Sheep have turned huge areas into quagmires that often extend into the park. But poaching is the curse of this no-man's-land. In 1983 a major local poaching ring was broken and wrists were slapped for the transportation of meat across interstate boundaries—but once a poacher's heaven, always so.

Tucked under the southwest corner of Yellowstone Park is the unusual 14,000-acre Winegar Hole Wilderness, geographically a continuation of the Bechler area, but really a bit of misplaced northern Minnesota. Probably the flattest wilderness in the state, it holds riches— swamps, marshes, forests and meadows—that cater to an elite population of grizzlies, trumpeter swans and loons. Closing the Grassy Lake road from Squirrel Meadows to Lake of the Woods would make ecological sense by establishing a completely roadless corridor between the two parks.

Gros Ventre Range

In complete contrast to the spectacular Tetons, breaking the east horizon of Jackson Hole is the much older Gros Ventre Range, composed chiefly of folded hard and soft sedimentary rocks.

As the Tetons attract the climbers of the world, the Gros Ventre Range beckons sportsmen to one of the finer hunting grounds of the continent. Fitting roughly into the parallelogram formed by four major rivers—Gros Ventre

(north), Snake (west), Hoback (south), and Green (east), it is about 25 miles square. With block-like, craggy, weathered summits and deeply scored and timbered gorges, it provides a vast area for exciting exploration by hikers. Bears and herds of elk, moose and mule deer roam the valleys and steep slopes, grizzlies wander in and out, and the trails of some 400 mountain sheep crisscross the sharp ridges and high peaks. This is the region through which the Jackson Hole elk herd traditionally migrated between their summer and winter ranges.

The name for the range came from the Gros Ventre (GROW-vont, French for "big bellies") Indians, a Blackfeet clan who hunted the area. The misnomer was applied to these athletically-built people because their nickname in plains sign language was a sweeping pass with both hands in front of the stomach, meaning "always hungry," or "beggars," which French trappers misread as "big bellies."

Paleo man hunted in the Gros Ventres when Pinedale glaciers still filled Jackson Hole. Traces of camps left by hunting teams of Indians can be found in these mountains, along the Gros Ventre River, in Jackson Hole, especially around Jackson Lake, and even in the Tetons themselves. Each spring entire Indian villages moved into the valley to follow the fishing, forage and hunting cycles, to look for obsidian and to enjoy the awe-inspiring scenery. Artifacts dating from as early as 12,000 years ago—tools, tepee rings and structures—were left as evidence. The fur trappers would follow Indians' trails into the country.

The values of the Gros Ventre Range are entirely different from those of the Tetons. Although not dramatic like the Tetons, the Gros Ventre scenery is spectacular—with peaks higher than 11,000', many with steep, sheer colorful cliff bands, glacially scoured cirque basins, high mountain lakes, and sloping valleys with numerous clear streams emanating in four geographical directions. Where the Teton rocks are patterns in black and white, the Gros Ventres are a collage of colorful rocks—bright reds, pinks, purples, grays and browns—splashed as cliffs, ridges, badlands. Here soft beds, the landslides and mudflows, have melted out and flowed down slopes like giant multi-colored masses of taffy. The southern Gros Ventres are gray and yellow tilted layers of snowcapped peaks.

Top: Thunderheads over Pinnacle Peak in the Gros Ventre Wilderness, Bridger-Teton National Forest. GEORGE WUERTHNER

Bottom: The Red Hills of the Gros Ventre Range. LORRAINE G. BONNEY

Top: The Gros Ventre Slide Geological Area on the Bridger-Teton National Forest. Bottom: The debris from the slide in the Gros Ventre River below Lower Slide Lake makes this a Class VI kayak run in high water. LORRAINE G. BONNEY PHOTOS

The Gros Ventres have been fashioned out of uplifted sedimentary formations—predominantly limestone and dolomite, suitable for climbing. Ancient inland seas deposited the stratified rock; upheavals thrust them skyward; Ice Age glaciers carved and scoured the mountains; erosion continues to shape the remaining heights from 9,000' to the 11,682' Doubletop Peak. The climbing is more like scrambling than in the Tetons, but where else can a climber relax luxuriously in Granite Hot Springs and, from a floating position, carefully study the mountaineering problem of perpendicular-walled Chimney Rock towering above the pool.

During the Laramide Orogeny the rooted Gros Ventre mountains were thrust south and southwest for three or four miles. The Overthrust mountains thrust east and northeast 50 to 75 miles and collided with the Gros Ventre Range near present-day Jackson.

For a study of earth movements, the exciting and colorful Gros Ventre River valley cannot be excelled, even by the Montana earthquake. Consider the 1925 Gros Ventre Slide: a mile-long mountain mass slid 2,000' into—and up the other side of—the valley in three minutes. There also are lessons in the Upper Gros Ventre Slide (1908-1912), the older slide scars of Slate, Dry Cottonwood and Goosewing Creeks, the Soda Lake and Bacon Ridge slide. The mud flows, tumbled masses and tilted living trees show spectacular shifts of the mountainsides and evidence of past landslides on a much larger scale. Still-collapsing, kettle-like topography probably results from dissolving gypsum creating collapse areas, or possibly suggests that buried glacial ice remnants continue to melt. The slowly shifting Gros Ventre River valley has long been a deterrent to road building, for good reasons. Early trappers followed the long-used Indian route through here into Jackson Hole, as did President Chester Arthur's Yellowstone-bound cavalcade in 1883.

The Gros Ventre Slide made headlines when, on June 23, 1925, the north ridge of Sheep Mountain tumbled into the Gros Ventre valley in less than three minutes, damming the river and creating Lower Slide Lake. The natural dam lasted two years, then saturation and water pressure burst it on May 18, 1927, with a tremendous flood that wiped out the village of Kelly, six miles downstream, and drowned six people. The livid gash the landslide made can be seen across the valley. Set aside as the Gros Ventre

Slide Geological Area, the area presents an awesome sight of giant boulders scattered across the valley like jumbled housetops after an earthquake.

After more than 20 years in the works, the Wyoming Wilderness Act of 1984 created the long-needed Gros Ventre Wilderness, protecting one of the last large undeveloped mountain ranges, with its richly diverse wildlife and some of the finest elk habitat in the area. The upper Gros Ventre River is one of the most beautiful and alive high mountain river valleys in the country, with probably some of the best moose habitat in the Lower 48. Unfortunately, wilderness boundaries weren't drawn with habitat in mind and the best wildlife habitat did not get into the wilderness. The fringe areas of the range form the conflict belt—where lower slopes break into quaking aspen country and sagebrush grasslands, the best winter range and calving areas. Such country is systematically left out of wilderness designation, like lower Tosi and Rock creeks down to the Green River. Rep. John Seiberling (D-OH) wanted it in wilderness. Rep. Dick Cheney (R-WY) wanted it in a special category that legislatively opened the area to logging. In the resulting deadlock, nothing was done.

Shoal Creek Wilderness Study Area, a major wildlife habitat, is an important part of that fringe area. North from Bondurant, the study area is the highly scenic terrain on the south flank of the Gros Ventre Mountains. Where the broad gently sloping timbered bench of the wilderness study area ends and the rocks begin, is where the Wyoming delegation placed the wilderness boundary until Rep. Seiberling was able to get Shoal Creek placed under wilderness study status. The Forest Service will re-examine the wilderness study areas during the preparation of its "second generation" management plan some 10 to 15 years hence.

The strikingly different compositions of three east-side summits of Jackson Hole intrigue any geologist. Jackson Peak (10,741'), east of the town of Jackson, is granitic gneiss like the Tetons. Eight miles north, Sheep Mountain (11,190'), also known as Sleeping Indian, is limestone, elevated from the floors of ancient seas. Mt. Leidy (10,326'), 14 miles farther north, is a stabilized heap of gravel aggregates like those on the floor of Jackson Hole, believed deposited 60 to 70 million years ago on top of Cretaceous sandstones which had already been folded and worn flat by erosion. The entire complex was then uplifted to this high mountain. Between Leidy and Sheep Mountain is the plastic earth of still-moving mudflows, slides and quake faulting.

Mt. Leidy Highlands

To the north of the Gros Ventre River are the Mount Leidy Highlands—long, rounded tree-covered ridges, dissected valley bottoms, wet, glaciated meadows, colorful arid badlands, steep, forested peaks topped by Mount Leidy, its 10,326' gravel summit highly visible from north Jackson Hole. Its vegetative diversity—a mosaic of coniferous forest, quaking aspen, alpine meadow and grassland—makes it top-quality elk habitat from the Gros Ventre River north to Togwotee Pass road, with spring and summer elk ranges, migration routes and calving grounds. Today only about 100,000 acres of it are still roadless.

The historic southern elk migration route before heavy settlement of the valley was from the Yellowstone-Teton wilderness area south through the Mount Leidy Highlands to wintering grounds in south Jackson Hole. Settlement of the Buffalo Fork, hunting in Grand Teton National Park, large-scale road building and clearcutting in Spread and Fish creeks and the Highlands in general, forced the elk westward. Their migration through Teton Park created major elk management problems. One by-product of these problems is an established hunt in Grand Teton National Park; it is the only hunt allowed in any U.S. national park. Interest has been expressed in attempting to re-establish the traditional elk migratory route through the western part of the Leidy Highlands, which would require allowing the land to revert to a wilder condition.

In February and March of 1985, Bridger-Teton National Forest officials fully intended to renew oil and gas leases, and thus permit new road construction and exploration in these same areas. Critical grizzly bear habitat, major elk migration routes, the east boundary of Grand Teton National Park, the Teton Science School and five dude ranches would have been drastically affected. This entire area north of the Gros Ventre River had been subjected to the Forest Service's unit planning process in the mid-1970s, before RARE II. It was recommended for extensive logging and road building. Only in the mid-1980s did some people realize that, despite all the timbering done there, an incredibly valuable wildland and still-roadless area remained.

Mt. Leidy, 10,326' high.
GEORGE WUERTHNER

Virtually all types of wildlife indigenous to the middle Rocky Mountains are found here, including the rare lynx, bobcat and mountain lion. The Sheridan National Recreation Trail and the Continental Divide National Scenic Trail both traverse the eastern portion.

Because the roadless areas are such a fount for precious and fast-disappearing habitat and wildlife, they have become the focus of an environmental storm as Jackson Hole residents, whose economy depends on these factors, protest the intensive oil, gas and timber mining of the surrounding areas.

37

Cirque and moraines in Gros Ventre Wilderness, with the Tetons beyond.
GEORGE WUERTHNER

The 3.4-million-acre empire of the Bridger-Teton National Forest is the largest and most controversial stand of federal trees in the Lower 48. It is also the arm and leg of that magnificent body of federal wilderness in northwest Wyoming called the Greater Yellowstone Ecosystem—a magnet that attracts 3 million visitors yearly, 1.5 percent of America's population, to Jackson Hole.

If any national forest in America should be the premier recreation, scenic and wildlife forest of the nation, it is the Bridger-Teton—where commodity outputs—timber, oil, gas—are dwarfed by recreation uses.

As a result of its location and attributes it is the center of tugs-of-war between those who would log its timber and drill for oil and gas, and those who would preserve it for guiding, sightseeing, hunting, backpacking and other recreation activities.

Because it is so important, the Bridger-Teton is a trendsetter, a testing ground, a bellwether forest. Managers of other national forests watch it to see what the issues are going to be down the road. The actions of Bridger-Teton make national headlines, and all because the people of Jackson Hole have been redefining their attitude toward the public lands around it, and for good reason, as we shall soon see.

In 1984, the "Wilderness Year," the 98th Congress designated 8.3 million acres of new wilderness in 20 bills, including a Wyoming Wilderness bill covering 884,049 new wilderness acres and 180,540 wilderness study acres.

Conversely, in 1985, the remaining millions of roadless RARE II acres were released which, like pressing the Go button on a game machine, triggered instant action. The release sent the Forest Service back to completing its critical 50-year forest management plans (that will be revised every 10 years), provoked a major struggle by the conservation movement to control roading and logging, and polarized interest groups along the lines of their perceptions of what a national forest should be.

Because of the contentious nature of the diverse users of the Bridger-Teton, the battle scenes have shifted from Forest Service offices into the courts and even into Congress.

Since the sixties, when the Forest Service permitted the wholesale devastation of national forests by large timber contractors, the Forest Service has built up the largest road system in the world—340,000 miles of road, seven times the interstate system—at a rate of 4,000 to 5,000 miles a year! A 1981-83 Forest Service review revealed it had exceeded its road construction goal by 320 percent. In contrast, trail construction and reconstruction was only 29 percent complete. Chief Forester Max Peterson and his deputy chief, Jeff Sermon, are not foresters by training; they are road engineers, which may help to explain the Forest Service road-building mania. Max Peterson, in 1984, when defending his agency against accusations that the Forest Service has adopted "bulldozer diplomacy," said road-building expenditures had declined since the Carter years, from $494 million then to $456 million today, and that the number of Forest Service road engineers had dipped by 56, to 1,308.

Yet a 1986 report prepared for the National Trails Coalition under Sierra Club supervision and called *National Forest Trails: Neglected and Disappearing*, tells a stark story. It states succinctly that "more and more trail users are being crowded onto fewer and fewer trails."

According to the report, between 1969 and 1983, trail use increased 132 percent, from 5.6 million visitor days to some 13 million in all national forests, yet trail building had peaked in the 1940s at 144,000 miles. Despite 20 million acres being added to the national forests between 1932 and 1950, trail building and maintenance dropped drastically and by 1974, the trail system was only two thirds what it had been 40 years earlier. In 1932 there were 3.2 miles of trails for each mile of road on national forests. In 1955, road miles exceeded trail miles for the first time. By 1983 there were three miles of road for every mile of trail.

Under the law, trails are supposed to share equal status with roads. Yet between 1980 and 1983, an average of 1,700 miles of road were built on national forests each year while only 513 miles of trail were added. Some trails were lost to roads built over them. Some of the new roads are in roadless areas, and "The Forest Service estimates that 700 to 900 miles of roads per year will be built in roadless areas in the next 10 years," according to the report.

The Forest Service doesn't have to come up with cost/benefit ratios as does the Corps of Engineers. The Forest Service subsidizes deficit timber sales by building roads to gain access to the timber. Each timber sale program on the Bridger-Teton results in a net loss of about $10.00 to taxpayers for every tree a logger cuts down. Timber sales push miles of open roads through elk calving grounds, migration routes and critical wildlife habitat.

As the battle over the wildlife habitat unfolds, the differences in regional economic philosophies become apparent. Take Jackson Hole, whose life blood is tourism. When its scenery is ruined, its wildlife herds and habitats gone, its forests and hills mined, then Jackson Hole will be finished.

In the last few years Jackson Holers have been looking at the public land in a new light. For example, management of the public forest resource has become a subject in the county commissioner races. The Little Granite case against Getty Oil brought about the change. Residents of Jackson Hole had accepted 130 wells drilled in Teton County and on the Bridger-Teton, but they objected strenuously to the 131st, the Getty well, which the Forest Service allowed to be drilled. A lawsuit resulted. Pressure from Jackson Hole constituents became so intense that even the commodity-oriented Wyoming delegation acted in outright opposition to oil and gas interests and put Little Granite Creek Canyon into Wilderness.

On July 30, 1985, the forest supervisor of Bridger-Teton decided to place on hold three large timber sales in the Mt. Leidy Highlands and in the Upper Green River country until the 50-year forest plan was completed.

In an unprecedented move, Louisiana-Pacific Corporation (L-P) filed an administrative appeal. Never before in the history of the Bridger-Teton had L-P had to deal with a situation in which concerns for wildlife habitat, recreational uses and a tourist-based economy were given status equal to that of the timber industry.

Another center of contention is the Union Pass area along the Continental Divide, where the north end of the Winds gives way to the softly undulating Seven Lakes area of big basins and numerous little lakes tied together by wet meadows and swamps. This once-lovely area receives heavy off-road vehicle use under the Forest Service's "management in a roadless condition."

But the big issue in the Union Pass area is a three-quarter-mile stretch of road which, if upgraded as Louisiana Pacific urges, would allow L-P trucks to get from Green River country over Union Pass to the L-P mill at Dubois. This would open the upper Green area and the eastern end of the Gros Ventres to timbering. As it is now, there is no easily driveable link either from the Gros Ventre valley or Green River basin into the Togwotee Pass or Wind River area. If that road building program is completed, the easily driveable link between the Gros Ventre Road and the Togwotee Pass highway would drastically increase vehicular traffic, facilitate timber sales, increase off-road vehicle use and poaching, and add further hunting pressure and all the other inherent problems that go along with increased road access.

THE OVERTHRUST BELT

Snake River Canyon.
LORRAINE G. BONNEY

Salt River Range at sunset.
GEORGE WUERTHNER

The Hoback-Wyoming and Snake River-Salt River ranges fill the southwest corner of Wyoming with their long, parallel, north-south trending mountain ridges. Although separated by river valleys, they are geologically part of the same mountain chain.

They are like two large dotted ii's (dots to the north) filling a rectangle in the southwest corner between Utah to the south and Teton Pass to the north. The western i, along the Wyoming-Idaho border, is the Salt River Range, severed from its dot, the Snake River Range, by the Snake River Canyon and U.S. Highway 26-89. Targhee National Forest manages the west side of the divides, Bridger-Teton the east. The eastern i is the Wyoming Range dotted by the Hoback Range lying north of the Hoback River and U.S. Highway 191-189. Greys River separates the two i's.

Structurally different from the central Wyoming uplifts, these mountains appear as crumpled, steeply tilted rock layers. They are sedimentary remnants of large folds pushed eastward across younger rocks by a series of low-angle thrusts from the west and southwest. The thrusts' intensity deformed the thick (as much as 90,000') section of sedimentary rocks into thrust plates that overlap from west to east. In other words, like a thick stack of heavily buttered pancakes, these great slabs of sedimentary rock skidded east some 50 to 75 miles into Wyoming. The "rootless" Overthrust Belt's slow movement took several million years and, in addition, was on a collision course with the Gros Ventre and ancestral Teton ranges in Jackson Hole near Jackson, Wyoming, and at Teton Pass. Geologists have yet to figure out whence came these slithery pancakes—Utah? Idaho? They haven't found a spot that matches. Also much debated is the source of the force that jolted the thrust belt into Wyoming and caused the foreland (other) ranges to rise.

During mid-Pliocene time, about 5 million years ago, the great freshwater Teewinot Lake filled Jackson Hole, and 25 miles southwest was another such lake, Grand Valley Lake. Although the lakes were on opposite sides of the Snake River Range, the ancestral Snake already had cut its canyon through to directly connect the lakes.

A total of 685,000 acres of potential wilderness was described in three of the four ranges by conservationists in the RARE II/Roadless Area studies. But the Wyoming congressional delegation proposed only one fifth of that

acreage as a Wilderness Study Area in its Wyoming Wilderness Act of 1984. According to a 1984 USGS study, the area is "highly favorable for the occurrence of oil and gas." The "winner," of temporary wilderness status as a Wilderness Study Area was the Palisades Area in the Snake River Range, a sensitive, rugged area of dense forest and unusually lush meadows. It is one of Wyoming's premier big game areas and today is blanketed with oil and gas leases.

Wilderness study area (WSA) status means that such areas be administered "...so as to maintain their presently existing wilderness character..." and yet the Wilderness Act guarantees "reasonable access" to explore for oil and gas in the Palisades. To Rep. John Seiberling of Ohio,

Overthrust features in the Hoback Peak area of the Wyoming Range (TOP, CHARLES FROIDERAUX) *and upper Game Creek* (BRIDGER-TETON N.F.)

author of the compromise Wyoming Wilderness Act, this meant that helicopters and other nonsurface-disturbing methods could be used in the sensitive Palisades area.

Bypassed as WSA's because of oil and gas potential were two other major Thrust Belt roadless areas, Grayback and Commissary ridges in the Wyoming Range. According to the Bridger-Teton National Forest Roadless Area Reevaluation Study, "the energy industry would like to see the area remain open to development."

Three rivers in the thrust belt are famous for their fishing and whitewater thrills. Greys River is a heart-thumper Class VI (or, nearly unnavigable) in high water; the Snake in its canyon is a challenger at any water level; and the Hoback has surfing waves any time.

Snake River Range

Idaho and Wyoming, as well as the Targhee and Bridger-Teton national forests, share the Snake River Range, whose outstanding qualities are masked from view by gentle foothills. But the range's rugged limestone-sandstone-shale crest culminates in 9,863' Powder Peak (Wyoming) and in 10,040' Mt. Baird (Idaho).

Third in size and elevation of the Overthrust group, the Snake River Range is the northern extension of the larger Salt River Range. From the Snake River Canyon its divide rises to Powder Peak then rolls northward to collide with the geologically different Teton structure at Teton Pass. All its streams drain into the Snake River, hence the name. In South Park, its spring and fall colors provide a breathtaking sweep of riotous flame and muted greens from Munger Mountain to Teton Pass.

This 22-mile-long forest of low peaks is famous for its hunting and fishing, its amazingly varied and dynamic gardens of wildflowers, its Snake River Canyon, the experience of solitude it provides, its powder bowl skiing at Teton Pass. Thanks to the "cloud-milking" habits of the pass, where precipitation is released as the clouds rise over it, Jackson Hole and the Gros Ventres are in the rain shadow of the Tetons, making Teton Pass an area abundant in Englemann spruce and subalpine fir.

The heart of the area, the 135,840-acre Palisades Wilderness Study Area, is surrounded by miles of deep canyons and steep ridges, and visited only by those willing to exert themselves. So close to Jackson Hole, yet visitors can tramp among the peaks for days at a time without

seeing other people. Rewards are spectacular views of the Tetons to the north, lush wildflowers at the bases of retreating snowbanks, the few twisted and stunted white-bark pines, fir and spruce dramatically contorted by the harsh elements, occasional glimpses of deer and elk on distant ridges, the incomparable experience of witnessing summer storms, sunrises and sunsets in solitude from lofty vistas.

The Palisades Wilderness Study Area has been under consideration for wilderness status since RARE I. Oil and gas leasing in the area led to the courtroom, and a controversial Sierra Club lawsuit decision ruled that any additional leasing be accompanied by an environmental impact statement because this unit was a further planning area in RARE II. If the Palisades ever is combined with the adjoining 125,000-acre proposed wilderness in Idaho, the result could be a stunning ecological entity of wildlife winter/summer ranges, watershed and plantlife.

Because of steep topography and weaknesses in the rock, slides are very common. One scree and talus slide in

The headwaters of Indian Creek in the Palisades Wilderness Study Area, Snake River Range, with the Tetons in the distance. GEORGE WUERTHNER

Facing page: Sunset on Murphy Creek in the Salt River Range, Bridger-Teton National Forest. GEORGE WUERTHNER

43

Snake River Range from Munger Mountain. LORRAINE G. BONNEY

Kayaking the Snake River at Jackson Hole. JEFF FOOTT

Blowout Canyon is three miles long and 1,000' to 1,500' wide, making it larger than the famed Gros Ventre Slide in Jackson Hole. This unstability has helped keep it from being logged.

The area has been hunted at least since Indian days. In his diary of 1837, early trapper Osborne Russell, hunting in Snake River Canyon, wrote, "Here we found immense numbers of Mountain Sheep which the snows drove down...we could see them nearly every morning from our lodges standing on the points of rock." Today they are reported occasionally, crowded out of this natural habitat by many factors, such as multitudes of domestic sheep on the western slopes of Targhee National Forest. Despite being heavily harvested for timber in the past, the Palisades's rugged terrain of dense forest and unusually lush meadows is prime habitat for elk, deer, moose, black bears, coyotes, cougars and bobcats.

It has numerous trails, two major ones and various approach trails that lead into the range via such main drainages as Black Canyon, Mill Creek, North and South Fall Creeks, Coburn, Dog, Wolf, and Red creeks. The Divide Trail follows the crest, indiscernible from crisscrossing elk trails between Starvation Peak and Observation Peak. The conflicting Sheep Driveway—lush in spring, devastated by sheep being driven through it in the fall—marches through the range following valleys and ridges, and adds to the confusion of following the Divide Trail where the trails meet.

The differences in philosophy between eastern Idaho sheepmen and western Wyoming cowboys was settled in 1886 when some hard-nosed sheepmen began bringing their flocks over Teton Pass. A warning signed by "the Settlers of Jackson's Hole," plus a bunch of dead-serious folks with guns turned them back. Somehow one determined bunch sneaked through and crossed the Snake over a bridge of end-to-end wagon beds covered with brush. After some 200 sheep were killed, the rest were escorted east out of the valley over Union Pass. Another such fracas occurred in 1901 at Mosquito Pass and the sheepmen got the message. The Jackson Holers, crowded out elsewhere by sheep, said the valley was too small for both sheep and cattle, and that's how it's been ever since.

Once at the summit of Hoback Rim, the historic pass between Pinedale and Jackson Hole via U.S. Highway 187-191, the road tips downward for the descent, and the traveler's eyes are greeted by a panoramic spectacle of the snow-patched rugged crest, steep slopes, rock cliffs, and talus falls of the Wyoming Range. Winter or summer, this approach to the 55-mile-long range is a thrill. Its fairly high altitudes range from 10,000' to 11,363' at Wyoming Peak, even though it rises only moderately above the 7,500' floor of Hoback Basin to the east.

The Wyoming Range

The Wyoming Range is the eastern segment and leading edge of the Thrust Belt. Although the northern end is quite majestic, as the uplift diminishes southward, the range becomes more accessible, and more interesting from an oil and gas standpoint.

Named after the creation of Wyoming Territory in 1868, the range rises between Greys River (west) and the Green River (east). Still considered wild and remote, these mountains are critical watershed for the Hoback and Snake rivers. The area contains remnant populations of Colorado cutthroat trout, classified "rare" by the state of Wyoming and "sensitive" by the U.S. Forest Service. The little-known Wyoming Range Recreation Trail bisects the entire length of the area. Big game hunting is important here; trophy hunts are popular due to the rugged terrain and extensive cover found on the north-facing slopes. President Theodore Roosevelt hunted in the Grayback early in this century. A successful mountain bighorn sheep reintroduction was completed in 1981.

The extremely steep west escarpment of the southern Wyoming Range drops impressively from the crest into Greys River. The east slope tends to have a rugged crest with long forested benches emanating down from the crest. Most of the east-flowing drainages have been re-lentlessly logged. In fact, for a horrible sight, fly over it—square clearcuts and roads everywhere. Only the great instability of the soil has prevented complete deforesta-tion of the benchland drainages. Heavy logging plus soil movement and slide activity like that found in several drainages, particularly Sheep Creek, contribute enor-mously to the turbidity of the Hoback in its spring rise.

The Wyoming Range had several large RARE II roadless areas including the southern Commissary Ridge and the northern Grayback Ridge. Unfortunately, being in the Overthrust Belt hasn't helped their cause.

Grayback Ridge was rated by the Bridger-Teton Forest

biologist as the second most important roadless area next to the Gros Ventre Wilderness. It was more than 200,000 acres in size, its high rugged peaks culminating in Hoback Peak at 10,862'. Its two subcrests, the northwest-southeast running Grayback Ridge, and the north-south crest, are separated by Willow Creek, the heart of the area. Willow Creek's entire drainage, down to its confluence with the

Grayback Ridge and Willow Creek in the Wyoming Range.
GEORGE WUERTHNER

45

South of Labarge Creek the Overthrust Mountains change names. The Wyoming Range becomes Commissary Ridge—an outstanding roadless area noted for its relict cutthroat trout in Bear River, and one of Wyoming's best reproducing Shiras moose herds on Hams Fork.

The terrain of the Lake Alice/ Commissary Ridge Roadless Area is characterized by massive ridges with fairly gentle tops, and steep slopes that plunge into the drainages, summer range for 2,500 elk. Mountain tops and many slopes are covered with fractured rock or limestone-sandstone-shale rock slides. The country is geologically older than the Salt River and the northern Wyoming ranges that have areas of well developed soils. Here too are large areas of natural slope instability. One lake, created by an ancient landslide dam, has no overland outlet; the water emerges in Spring Lake Creek a half mile below the lake.

Although studied by the Bureau of Land Management as a Wilderness Study Area, the 13,970-acre Lake Mountain Area did not receive wilderness status. The area is noted for its rare breed of genetically pure Colorado River cutthroat in Rock Creek, and as winter range for one of the last naturally wintering elk herds.

This area was trapped extensively during the 1830s. The Lander Cutoff of the Oregon Trail passed north of this roadless area, marked by an early gravesite located in Upper Hobble Creek. Old cabins and shacks, remnants of early grazing periods, exist, as do sheepherder carvings and graffiti. Tie hack cabins are still found, dating from the turn of the century when ties were cut for the railroads.

The Hoback Range

The Hoback Range, from Hoback River Canyon north to the Snow King Mountain area, is the northern extension of the Wyoming Range, but cut off from it by the Hoback River. It forms the eastern fringe of South Park and provides the colorful backdrop to the town of Jackson. Lowest and smallest of the Thrust group, it is often considered part of the Gros Ventre Range because it was squashed against the southwest corner of that range when the Thrust Belt collided with the Gros Ventres back in the Laramide Orogeny.

Trappers following the old Indian trail through Hoback Canyon along the Hoback's flanks had to cross the Red

Whitebark pine frames Hoback Peak near Cliff Creek Pass in the Wyoming Range. GEORGE WUERTHNER

critical upper drainages of Little Greys, Cliff Creek, and the Hoback—all partially roadless in their upper reaches. Since the Wyoming Wilderness Act of 1984, the Forest Service has proposed timber sales in several of the fringe drainages, and oil and gas leases within the area. Chevron is drilling above Cliff Creek, its rig right below Deadman Peak. Many little inroads are eroding and slowly shrinking this huge roadless area.

Howie Wolke, co-founder of the Earth First! environmentalist organization, chose to defend this wilderness with civil disobedience. Wolke spent six months behind bars and paid a fine of $3,304 for removing survey stakes being used to lay out an access road to the Chevron Oil rig.

46

Ledges (Nugget Sandstone), an exposed area 200' above the river. Many of the trappers lost their pack stock here. W.A. Ferris, in 1832, described his ordeal through this section: "we all dismounted, and led our animals over the most dangerous places, but...three of them lost their footing, and were precipitated into the river below. Two were... slightly injured, having fortunately fallen on their loads...but the other was killed instantly." Wilson Price Hunt, Nathaniel Wyeth, Osborne Russell, Robert Stuart, Rev. Samuel Parker all described the dangerous spot.

Where the Hoback River flows into the Snake at Hoback junction, U.S. Highway 26-89-191 heads north into Jackson, passing west of the Hoodoos. Weird erosions are etched by wind and water in Hoback sedimentaries, roosting area for raptors.

The Hoback Range benefited when Ohio's Rep. John Seiberling heard the local cry of outrage over nearby mineral leasing. Because of him the Gros Ventre Wilderness gained two critical additions near Jackson Hole, the 41,000-acre Little Granite/Horse Creek addition, and the 17,500-acre Twin Creek/Cache and Sheep Mountain sections of the Hoback Range.

The Salt River Range

The mountain road of U.S. Highway 89 from Evanston north to Jackson Hole plays tag with the Wyoming-Idaho border along the west flank of the fault-blocked Salt River Range, most impressive of the Overthrust Mountains.

Bounded by the Grand Canyon of the Snake River (north), Star Valley and Salt River to the west, and separated from the Wyoming Range (east) by Greys River, the 150-mile-long Salt River Range rises from 6,600' to its highest point, Rock Lake Peak, at 10,763'.

This classically rugged north-south range, with steep drainages flowing west and east, forms the hydrographic divide between the Salt River and Greys River. Its western escarpment is steep and rugged. The eastern side has high glacier cirques, which tend to drop off into long ridges or forested benches that slope into Greys River. The Forest Service has logged off every drainage on the east side with the exception of Cow and Corral creeks.

The major drainages, with steep, rugged, narrow canyons, are a common feature along the valley front. Large faults are present throughout, creating high vertical cliffs and rock walls, with many elevations over 10,000'.

Haystack Mountain on Strawberry Creek in the Salt River Range.
HOWIE WOLKE

Like the rest of the thrust group, the Salt River Range's excellent habitat is rich in wildlife—elk, deer, bear, moose, coyote, lynx, bobcat, mountain lion—with many important elk calving areas. Greys River has consistently produced some of the biggest trophy mule deer in the state. The elk herd summers throughout the high country of the entire thrust belt, usually dropping into Star Valley to winter on the Wyoming Department of Game and Fish grounds there. Many elk used to migrate down to the Red Desert with the antelope until the migration routes were cut off. The north-facing slopes are predominantly a mixture of Douglas fir, Englemann spruce and subalpine fir. The range supports plant communities of Rocky

47

Mountain spruce/fir, Douglas fir and Rocky Mountain sagebrush steppe, all in short supply in the national wilderness system.

The Salt River Range's special attraction is a geological feature called Periodic Spring, which floods its cave every 18 minutes. It is the largest of three cold-water geysers known in the world.

Because the range is in the Overthrust Belt, its geology is complex, and gas and oil leases puncture most of the area, although there had been no initial production from the five wells drilled up to 1983.

Star Valley—with the Salt River Range in the background—is Wyoming's westernmost large valley, shared with Idaho. The Salt River flows here, a clear, sweet river with great fishing despite its name. The name comes from the salt flats several miles west near Freedom, Idaho, where emigrants on the Lander Cutoff of the Oregon Trail in 1849 renewed their salt supplies. The Salt River emerges as a small stream from the southern Salt River Range, but swells from valley springs flowing into it. Large alluvial fans that slope from the range act as aquifers,

Facing page, far left: Red tilted layers of sedimentary rock on Battle Mountain in Hoback Canyon. KENT & DONNA DANNEN
Near left: Crest of the Salt River Range seen from Prater Mountain.
GEORGE WUERTHNER

This page, inset: Fish fossil 40 to 65 million years old, found at Fossil Butte National Monument. KENT & DONNA DANNEN
Right: Sandstone boulder at Fossil Butte National Monument. JEFF GNASS

storing excess groundwater and stabilizing the river flow in the spring runoff.

South of Labarge Creek this range has various local names including Tump and Bear River Divide. The most westerly is the Sublette Range, where the Bureau of Land Management identified a sliver of wilderness surrounding Raymond Mountain, their 32,936-acre Raymond Mountain Wilderness Study Area, just off the southwest corner of the Bridger-Teton National Forest and about 25 miles northwest of Kemmerer. Here, in one of its several streams of this oasis, lurks a pure strain of Utah cutthroat. In addition, the area is important moose, deer and elk habitat. It has steep topography, lovely forests and parks, great botanical diversity that includes a magnificent wildflower display, unusual geologic formations and great scenic viewpoints, all in boomtown Kemmerer's backyard.

After the westward transcontinental trails converged through South Pass, most of them angled toward the south end of the Salt River Range, crossing near Kemmerer (Overland Stage Route, Sublette Cutoff), and old Fort Bridger near Evanston (the California, Overland, Mormon, and Oregon trails and the original route of the Pony Express.

Ten miles west of Kemmerer the 8,180-acre Fossil Butte National Monument, established in 1972, rises a thousand feet above the valley, where an unusually rich concentration of fossil fish vertebrates are entombed in a three-foot-deep layer of limestone, found 30' to 300' below the surfaces of the butte.

THE WIND RIVER RANGE

Alpine laurel contrasts with the oldest Precambrian rock known, found in the Wind River Range.
PAT O'HARA

War Bonnet and Warrior I in the Southern Winds tower above Jackass Pass, one of the half dozen ways to cross the Continental Divide in the Wind River Range.
JEFF GNASS

The enormous mountain uplift called the Wind River Range is the supreme expression in Wyoming of the Laramide Orogeny. These "Shining Mountains" of early Indians and Spanish conquistadores straddle the Continental Divide for a hundred miles, making this range the highest, largest, wildest, and most awesome in Wyoming. Officially starting at Togwotee Pass and U.S. Highway 287 on the north, the "Winds," as the range is affectionately called, stretch southeasterly to South Pass, an unbroken, 100-mile barrier between central and western Wyoming.

The Winds are visually one of Wyoming's best kept secrets. Few of the 45 peaks above 13,000' can be seen from the highways circling the range. From the west, U.S. Highway 191 gives only brief glimpses of the range's glories through the haze of distance and foothills. From the east, visitors driving U.S. Highway 287 along the eastern base of the range may never suspect the existence of the awesome, glacier-draped crest lying just 10 to 20 miles west behind the formidable curtain of foothills.

The Winds are special because of geology, glaciers, bighorns, and wilderness.

In "some of the greatest localized vertical displacement known anywhere in the world," according to Wyoming's eminent geologist Dave Love, the enormous compression of the Laramide Orogeny exerted full force into the 120-mile-long Wind River thrust fault, elevating the Winds above the surrounding landscape. They shedded thousands of feet of mantling sediments as they rose. The range was folded so severely that the rocks in essence "broke" and the fold was faulted over itself on the southwest side of the range.

This mighty thrust southwestward onto Green River Basin along a 45-degree fracture plane left the range with no west flank of sedimentary rocks, resulting in a 100-mile-long stretch of lime-deficient rocks. This significant lack of calcium shows up in the poor teeth of people living here and the lime-deficient characteristics of both domestic and wild animals.

What goes up must come down, and in the battle between orogeny and erosion, erosion always wins. Erosive forces worked on each new layer exposed during the uplift, removing thousands of feet of covering sediment until the ancient granite core was cleaned off and exposed right down to the oldest Precambrian rock known to exist— Early Archean. After 30 million years of erosion the

range was being slowly buried in its own discarded rubble. The tremendous blowout of debris from the Absaroka-Yellowstone area helped finish the burial, and the area was leveled to an undulating Miocene plain— with Wyoming's proudest poking through as a low range of 4,000' bulges.

Whence it came is still being debated, but a massive general upheaval swiftly lifted the interred mountains about a mile and started the monumental Exhumation of the Rockies. Streams were reactivated and began the vigorous corrosive process that would, with the help of the glaciers, produce today's topography.

During the ice ages northwest Wyoming was covered by glaciers of local origin. The margin of continental ice stayed to the north. The Wind River Range was part of the largest separate glaciated area south of the continental ice cap in the western United States. An immense ice cap 90 miles long and 20 to 30 miles wide formed along the

Mt. Hooker of the Wind River Range, in the Popo Agie Wilderness.
GEORGE WUERTHNER

51

Winds' crest, thick tongues of ice reaming their way down all the major canyons. In the ensuing centuries, glaciers advanced and receded five or so times as the climate changed, each ice sheet leaving its mark, each weaker and advancing less. These tremendous rivers of ice, some 3,000' thick, scraped away the softer rocks and bulldozed large canyons. The harder rocks, defying nature's earth-moving machines, remained as peaks, and only five passes traversable by horses transect the 100-mile-long backbone of the range. Today some 50 peaks and pinnacles in the Winds thrust their sharp summits above seven of the 10 largest glaciers of the lower 48 states. The ultimate is the glacier-draped summit of Gannett Peak, at 13,804' the highest peak in the state.

Today 63 glaciers in the range total 17 square miles. The majority are found in a narrow belt along the east side of the Continental Divide, with the greatest concentration in the north half of the Fitzpatrick Wilderness. The "Big Seven" glaciers range in size from 393 to 1,130 acres. (Interestingly, Wind River glaciers cover an area larger than all other Rocky Mountain glaciers put together.) Gannett Glacier, on the northeast slope of Gannett Peak, is the largest at 1,130 acres or 1.77 square miles (in 1950). The most frequently visited, Dinwoody Glacier, on the southeast side of Gannett Peak, is the fifth largest in the group, at 1.34 square miles.

In the 12 miles between Knife Point Mountain and Gannett Peak, the Continental Divide crest is an almost continual knife-edged ridge with many cirques eroded into its eastern side. Other landforms are fault zones, escarpments, talus slopes. The straight and precipitous western side of the summit ridge may be an escarpment, result of the ridge being faulted upward. This would explain its prominence above the old peneplane surfaces. The 12,000'-high peneplanes, those particularly noticeable undulating plateaus above-timberline—Goat Flat, Horse Ridge, Ram Flat—are remnants of the ancient eroded surface. They are level and covered with tundra-type vegetation, frost-shattered rock, and occasional rock rings, four to six feet in diameter that have been formed by frost action.

The sedimentary layers that once covered the granitic core were stripped from the mountains in all but the White Rock area near Green River Lake. Granite fragments along the range's east-sloping flank were left exposed in a series of hogbacks. This flank is paralleled for 60 miles by a series of classic anticlinal folds, which can be seen from U.S. Highway 287. They include today's oil-producing Derby Dome, and Dallas Dome where discovery of oil in commercial quantities was made in 1884.

Several caves in the Winds are found on this northeastern flank, such as the popular "sinks" of Sinks Canyon near Lander, where the Popo Agie River, cascading out of the range, almost turns on itself and plunges into a cave, to appear again half a mile below.

Because it was the Continental Divide, this great range fascinated early explorers like General John C. Fremont and Captain B.L.E. Bonneville. The latter knew more about the Wind River Range than most mountain enthusiasts today. He traveled their complete length on both flanks, circled the southern half through South Pass at least five times, made one complete circuit going north through Union Pass, and camped for long periods on both the Green and Popo Agie rivers. A soldier and keen observer, he was not idly boasting when he pointed out Gannett Peak as the one he had reached "upon that dividing ridge which the Indians regard as the crest of the world." The 37-year-old Bonneville approached and climbed Gannett in September 1833, from the east side, by following the long Horse Ridge ramp to its dead-end cliff overlooking the magnificent Dinwoody Glacier cirque. He had to retreat a little to descend to the glacier, which he crossed to climb Wyoming's highest summit.

Likewise General Fremont, aiming to climb the highest "Snow Peak" in the range, approached Gannett Peak from the south (Island Lake). On August 15, 1842, he mistakenly climbed a closer "Snow Peak," Mt. Woodrow Wilson (later so named because it seemed to have 14 points). From Island Lake, Wilson's bulk hid Gannett from view except for its snowy summit, which blended so perfectly with Wilson's that they appeared as one peak with little difference in elevation.

Gannett Peak is 25 trail miles from any roadhead. Yet for all the mountain's ruggedness, there are gradual trails through meadows and timber, along meandering streams in canyon bottoms, that lead into the heart of the wilderness without steep hiking. In one day you can reach campsites with superb scenery and excellent fishing.

An exhilarating approach to Gannett is Captain Bonneville's route—a 12-mile hike on the long, gently rising plateau of Horse Ridge. From Cold Springs, the dramatic

route starts through the Wind River Indian Reservation (permission and fee required). Soon both sides of the narrowing ridge drop off abruptly into glacial canyons so deep the bottom cannot be seen. Each mile teasingly reveals more rugged peaks, more sparkling ice until the southern end of Horse Ridge (13,000') dead-ends abruptly near the crumbling landmark of Chimney Rock.

Ahead is one of the most outstanding panoramic viewpoints in the mountain world—the great cirque of Dinwoody Glacier where glacier-shrouded matterhorns of the Continental Divide rise up to the king, Gannett Peak; where shining dirt-streaked glaciers, bergschrunds, and wicked crevasses seem almost within reach. Gannett Peak, named for Henry Gannett of the U.S.G.S., can be studied and admired in all its splendor, here where the Continental Divide seems worthy of its name as the

The long, undulating peneplane plateau remnant of Horse Ridge forms the skyline in this scene.
HOWIE WOLKE

Facing page: Gannett Peak with its striking glacier crest, as seen from Fremont Peak. The Sphinx (fore-peak) and the Divide peaks of Dinwoody, Doublet, the Dames Anglaises and Mt. Warren flank Gannett on the right.
GEORGE WUERTHNER

are protected in a natural state by three congressionally-created wilderness areas and the de facto wilderness of the Wind River Indian Reservation. Of these, the Bridger Wilderness twists along the west side of the divide for 80 miles. East of the divide, the reservation's 200,000 acres, designated a primitive area, are sandwiched between the Popo Agie Area to the south (pronounced po-POZ-yuh; in Crow Indian language, *agie* = river; *popo* = head; hence—headwaters) and the Fitzpatrick (formerly Glacier) Wilderness to the north. The latter includes the Whiskey Mountain natural winter range for the largest single herd of bighorn sheep in the world.

Despite the harsh climate of the great Wind River wilderness, it has a rich diversity of wildlife species ranging from big-game animals (moose, elk, sheep, mule deer) to smaller mammals (badger, yellow-bellied marmot, pika, red fox, marten, mink). It is black bear habitat, but a rare grizzly bear can wander in. A few mountain lions and numerous coyotes inhabit the area. Some 15 to 20 bird species can be found, but of the winged creatures, mosquitoes thrive the best.

The high snowfields of the Wind River Range give birth to the headwaters of some of the nation's great rivers. The Green River, on the official list of potential wild and scenic rivers, begins in the snow melt of Gannett's west-side Mammoth Glacier. Its icy waters cascade northward, recharging the popular Green River Lakes before its prime fishing waters hook around the Big Bend and flow south to join the Colorado on its way to the Gulf of California. Captain Bonneville was first to point out the Green's trick geography on his map, the first charting of Wyoming mountains based on actual knowledge.

East of the divide, the historic Sweetwater River—named by General William H. Ashley in 1924 and main western route of the immigrants—rises in the southern Winds, flows east into the North Platte River and ultimately empties into the Gulf of Mexico. The Wind River drains these mountains on the northeast, and flows into the Missouri-Mississippi River system.

Historically, the Bridger Wilderness had no fish in its hundreds of lakes until the successful stocking programs of the 1920s and 1930s. Today's fisherman can find six trout species, grayling and mountain whitefish, some of them of record size.

Unfortunately, recent Environmental Protection Agency studies concluded that these magnificent mountains in the heart of Wyoming, and especially the high wilderness lakes, are susceptible to damages from acid rain due to their low alkalinity, or ability to buffer sulfides and nitrates. The Winds are downwind of the coal-fired Jim Bridger steam electric plant northeast of Rock Springs. A yellow plume containing sulphuric acid sails north to drape itself over the Winds like egg yolk.

Piled on top of the "egg yolk" is the trona haze from Green River town's trona refinery. Trona—sodium sesquicarbonate—found in beds in the long-gone Lake Gosiute of Green River Basin, is an important component of many products, including glass. More than two tons of trona are dumped daily into the Green River simply from washing of the freight cars. So today the Green River is loaded with fluorine and trona which, to date, has had three drastic effects wherever used. It turned the land irrigated by the now-abandoned Lyman irrigation project on Blacks Fork River in southwestern Wyoming into soured alkali flats. So much trona dissolves naturally or is being dumped into the Green that the Colorado reservoirs downstream—lakes Powell and Mead—are being turned into chemical soups. Already Wyoming's southwest is considered a stroke and hypertension belt. If the trans-basin diversion of the Green ever goes through to the Powder River Basin, the Sweetwater-Platte-Powder River lands likely will become alkali flats too.

DESERT MOUNTAINS

Red sandstone gave the Red Desert its local name; officially, the area is the Continental Divide Basin.
KENT & DONNA DANNEN

The Sweetwater River, with the Granite Mountains for background.
W. R. HANSEN

To include a basin in a book on mountains is anomalous, but the Wyoming Basin, the "Great American Desert" is special—a complex system of lower granite mountains and basins surrounded by the impressive Middle Rocky Mountains to the north and west, and the Southern Rockies to the south and east. The Wyoming Basin has a most remarkable geologic feature, the Granite Mountains Uplift. This broad northwest-southeast trending uplift, the second largest granite-cored mountain uplift in Wyoming, stretches from the Wind River Range east 100 miles almost to the Laramie Range, in a series of desert ranges strung along its southern flank.

Had the geologic fate of the Granite Mountains Uplift been the same as that of other ranges including the neighboring Wind Rivers, it might have been a climbing area to rival the Winds, or another barrier to west coast travelers. Instead, because of geologic vagaries, it became a major travel route, its famous landmarks highlighting the long, tiresome trek westward, its buried granite domes a geologist's paradise.

Mostly bare or sage-covered, these semi-arid desert mountains rise from the sand and alkali of the Wyoming Basin. Many are flanked by large living sand dunes. If you listen closely, you can still hear the creaking wheels of the wagon trains headed west as they pass the historic landmarks of the Oregon Trail, the hideouts of the legendary badmen and where Cattle Kate did her pathetic dance at the end of a length of hemp. The pioneers have long since passed through, but the spirit of the frontier still haunts this weird landscape of granite domes and desert flats.

Why was it the 19th century "tourist delight"? Fremont's 1846 map was the first to show "ridges and masses of naked granite destitute of vegetation" along and north of the Sweetwater River. The old Oregon Trail, used by early trappers, Oregon settlers, Mormons and California gold seekers, followed the "mile wide and a foot deep" North Platte River to the Sweetwater River Crossing with its more potable, less alkaline waters. South of the stream rose the Green and Ferris mountains. Excitement quickened the pace up the Sweetwater as the new wave of tourists paraded past the landmarks of the Granite Mountains—Independence Rock, named Register of the Desert in 1840 by Father De Smet; Devils Gate, Split Rock, and Ice Slough, a boggy area where the travelers quarried ice, the persistent permafrost remnants of the Ice Age, all made famous

W. H. Jackson photo of the Hayden Expedition camping along the Sweetwater below Split Rock in 1872. The bottom of the split is a soft mafic Precambrian dike intruded along a fracture in the harder granite.
COURTESY U.S. GEOLOGICAL SURVEY

in dozens of pioneer journals and diaries. Ahead they could see Continental Peak and Oregon Buttes, giant announcements of South Pass on the Continental Divide.

Why a geologist's delight? Because the more than 3,000 square miles of the wedge-shaped complex called the Granite Mountains Uplift provides answers to certain geologic puzzles. This structure, today marked by a number of low hills and mountains—Granite, Green, Ferris, Seminoe and Shirley mountains—was thrust up westward in several stages as a single giant Laramide mountain range, 100 miles long and 30 miles wide, a block almost as big and high as the existing Wind River Range of early Tertiary time. Then, after volcanic debris blanketed Wyoming, the range collapsed, literally swallowed by the earth, sinking 3,000' or 4,000' as its Precambrian core was downdropped by faults on both sides. From then on it became the local "garbage pit" into which fell the debris from other uplifts. As these were hoisted high and tilted northward, the northward-flowing streams stripped off

their rocks, pushed them north across the buried Seminoe Mountains and dumped the debris on the already foundering Granite Mountains.

While most of Wyoming was undergoing vigorous erosion as the result of a broad general uplift that raised the land surface of Wyoming a mile, the Granite Mountains block kept right on sinking along the Split Rock syncline, dropping more than 1,000'. Moonstone Lake filled the depression, the higher knobs of granite protruding above the lake surface. During early Pleistocene time (3 million years ago) the Sweetwater River established itself along the trough of the Split Rock depression. It lost its erosive power as the Granites continued to sag. The sluggish river became trapped along a superimposed course across granite knobs, and was able to exhume only 1,000' of the buried crests of the Granite Mountains. Because of this, a remarkably complete record of sedimentation and tectonism, the progressive burial of this mountain range during the last 60 million years, has been preserved, recording what had been stripped off adjacent mountain ranges.

Why the miner's delight? Because the area has been rich in minerals. Nephrite jade was discovered in 1939. When word spread in lapidary circles, the hunt for jade intensified until in the 1950s thousands were combing the area. As the finds declined, the price of jade rose.

Sweetwater moss agates are found here, as are rubies and sapphires. Uranium, gold, silver, lead, copper, molybdenum, coal, iron and chromium, gas and oil are other minerals that have been mined in this region. The largest, most numerous, most productive uranium mines in the Granite Mountains area are in the Gas Hills district, 40 miles southeast of Riverton.

Within the semi-arid Wyoming empire of the Bureau of Land Management lie 44 gems, which the bureau selected as being worthy of wilderness study area status. None of them has survived the process of wilderness creation and the BLM is currently restudying several of the less controversial ones.

Within or near the Granite Mountains Uplift were found eight areas eligible for wilderness study—Oregon Buttes, Ferris Mountains, Sweetwater Canyon, four areas in the Sweetwater Rocks, and Bennett Mountains—with attractions varying from extremely rugged terrain, deep canyons and steep slopes, the sight of golden eagles and peregrine falcons. All have outstanding opportunities for solitude. Natural springs, moving sand dunes, climbing and rock-hounding areas, historical, geological and archaeological sites would combine to provide an exceptional wilderness experience in the desert mountains.

These exceptionally scenic mountains contain reddish granitic boulders, slabs and exfoliating domes interlaced with green wooded pockets of limber pine and juniper, freshwater floodplain meadows, and sagebrush/grassland habitat. The four units of Sweetwater Wilderness Study Areas—Lankin Dome, Split Rock, Savage Peak and Miller Springs—a total of 32,175 acres have excellent mule deer and bighorn habitat with escape and lambing areas. They are all on BLM land between Independence Rock and Jeffrey City—trailer town with a variable population of several hundred people, some 60 miles north of Rawlins.

The Granite Mountains

The Granite Mountains were described by Endlich of the 1879 Hayden Survey: "The absolute nakedness of these hills is truly remarkable. Without any definite rock structure they rise directly from the plain, presenting their bald, gray and red forms, which rise to a relative elevation of 300' to 1,100'. Smooth rounded surfaces of considerable extent render the ascent of some of the higher peaks almost an impossibility."

The exhumed granite of these mountains provides an exciting setting for the rock climber. Their remote location in the rain shadow of the Wind River Range, locked in by private property, has left them almost untouched by the climber's boot. The fairly homogenous granite forms textbook examples of exfoliated domes, calling for either continuous crack climbing or offering smooth friction slabs—truly a climber's heaven.

All these peaks—MacIntosh, Whiskey, Moonstone, Great Stone Face, Split Rock, Lankin Dome—are massive Precambrian granite monoliths. The prominent Lankin Dome, at the west end of the Granite Rocks, reminds one of Devils Tower. Its top is 1,400' above the foreground of Moonstone formation. Its 1,000' granite face has numerous possibilities for severe friction climbs on rough rounded granite containing large feldspar and mica crystals. The higher MacIntosh Peak has been exposed since Eocene times. Split Rock and Moonstone Peak have only recently been exhumed from complete burial.

Split Rock (7,305') a highly fractured peak, displays almost unmodified Miocene and Pliocene topography exhumed during Quaternary time. It is split by a soft black Precambrian dike that has eroded away, leaving a "split" like a gunsight notch between two high granite knobs. Its face offers superb climbing problems.

Devils Gate is one of the finest examples to be found anywhere of what a superimposed stream can do to resistant granite. After the Granite Mountains were buried by the sediment blanket, drainage systems were superimposed on the blanket, resulting in several odd river patterns. For example, after the Sweetwater River moved into the nearby trough line of the Split Rock syncline it eventually wore its way down through the sediment blanket to expose the buried mountain crest below. Thus let down and superimposed on top of this structure, and trapped on its route across the hard granite, the Sweetwater slowly eroded Devils Gate. Had the river been only three fourths of a mile south, it would have missed the granite completely. The vertical walls and elevator-shaft depression in the east buttress of Devils Gate present excellent climbing problems.

Prehistoric people, small bands of nomadic hunters and gatherers, frequented this region for at least 12,000 years. Near Split Rock a possible drive line and butchering site was located, with stone cairns, stone rings and logs that were apparently used to block escape routes. Butchering tools (choppers, bifaces) also were found here. In Sweetwater Canyon 13 prehistoric sites have been identified, probably used as occupation sites for short periods. They include a small area along the river floodplain consisting of several stone circles or tepee rings. A recently discov-

Independence Rock. "Black Robe" Father Pierre Jean De Smet found carved about the base of this rock the names of early mountain men and explorers. RON MAMOT

Facing page: Devils Gate, 19th century highlight on the Oregon Trail— also known as "Devils Door" in the 1840s—is an impressive gash cut through the rock formation by the Sweetwater River. RON MAMOT

A concentration of uranium mines is centered about Green Mountain.
RON MAMOT

The Bennetts contain a Wilderness Study Area. BUREAU OF LAND MANAGEMENT

ered site along the Sweetwater indicates habitation by prehistoric groups on a more permanent basis—several pithouse-style, semi-subterranean dwellings were used for an extended period of time about 5,700 years ago.

The first white men to visit the canyon were 11 fur trappers led by Jedediah Smith, including Bill Sublette, Tom Fitzpatrick and James Clyman. Given directions by the Crows, the group was headed over South Pass to the Green River to trap for Ashley and Henry's Rocky Mountain Fur Company. A severe winter storm stopped them near South Pass. They turned east down the Sweetwater, found shelter in a canyon with aspen groves and stayed there two or three weeks during February and March of 1824. Leaving a cache of powder and lead, they took off for a successful season of trapping. They returned about June 1, dug up the cache, and headed east.

Sweetwater Canyon begins at 7,150' in elevation and drops 430' (45 feet per mile) through the 9,056-acre wilderness study area. The canyon is a water-carved fault trough nearly 500' deep. In places the walls are almost vertical. Throughout the canyon, bare rock outcrops are interspersed with sagebrush, grasses, other shrubs, and pockets of aspen and willow. The topography and vegetation of the canyon are abrupt and striking, in contrast to the surrounding rolling hills.

Breeding waterfowl are common in the wet meadows of the Sweetwater, which itself has good brown and rainbow trout populations and the clearest, finest water in the Wyoming Basin. Transbasin diversion of water is being contemplated in Wyoming which could adversely modify the Sweetwater River for the native flora and fauna. It has

three plant communities not represented in the National Wilderness Preservation System—floodplain meadows, big sagebrush-grassland, and dry conifer woodlands. Bobcats, mountain lions, golden eagles, elk and mule deer have been seen in the pine-juniper woodlands nearby.

The Sweetwater Canyon segment of the Sweetwater River was denied status in the National Wild and Scenic River System in 1979 because it is only 6.5 miles long. It failed to meet minimum length requirement of 25 miles despite qualifying in every other way: It is free-flowing and has excellent wildlife values, water quality and outstanding historical values.

Placer gold was discovered in the area in 1842. Hard-rock gold mining began in 1867, with the discovery of the Carissa Lode, which caused a short-lived mining boom. Most of the mines were shut down by 1895.

If the Granite Range was raised along its bounding faults to its original height, it would be as high as the Winds are now. Its downdropped, buried core is far below the level of the satellite mountains that were uplifted and folded out of its flanking sediments. Every cluster of low hills has a local name, yet all are structurally part of the same range.

Starting in the west, the Granites are north of the Sweetwater River. The Green, Ferris and Seminoe/Haystack mountains are south of the Sweetwater and west of the North Platte River/Pathfinder-Seminoe reservoirs. On the Continental Divide, they form the north and east, or Atlantic, rim of the Great Divide Basin. The Pedro/Bennett, Shirley mountains and Freezeout Hills are east of the North Platte and form the western and southern horizons of Shirley Basin. Some have granite cores but most are the folded sedimentaries that once covered the granite core of the Granite Mountains Uplift.

The Green Mountains

Green Mountain (7,500' to 9,025'), sits on the Continental Divide north of the Great Divide Basin, bounded on the east by U.S. Highway 287 and Muddy Gap, 46 miles north of Rawlins. It extends 25 miles westward, paralleling U.S. Highway 287 and the Sweetwater River which bounds it on the north. Crooks Creek was superimposed on the Green Mountain topography to form Crooks Gap. Mostly sandstone with some limestone, shale, granite and metamorphics, it has been the scene of much uranium prospecting. In fact, these mountains have been riddled by a maze of roads and mining scars that are amazing to see. The source of the host rock was the granitic core of the Granite Mountains.

The Ferris Mountains

Just east across U.S. Highway 287 is the 10,037' Continental Divide summit of Ferris Mountain, perched 3,000' above Separation Flats and the Ferris dune fields. In the 16th century, according to legend, Spaniards came north and prospected the Spanish mine area in the Ferris Mountains. Its striking white scallops or "flatirons" on the southern flank, seen from U.S. Highway 287, are vertical beds of limestone that have resisted erosion, an outstanding scenic feature that can be seen for miles. The proposed Continental Divide Trail will pass below these arches. To reach Ferris Peak looks simple enough but this rugged little range requires some unbelievable bushwhacking.

The Ferris dune field to the south has migrating Quaternary sand dunes, one of which has covered a small lake and is in the process of exposing a previous lake. A high water table supports the vegetation, mostly Indian rice grass, which in turn stabilizes the sand. When the vegetative cover is disturbed by wind or man, the dunes shift and reform. Winds here have been clocked at some of the highest speeds ever recorded in the continental U.S. Nearby Sand Creek is a superimposed drainage, cutting deep water gaps. Muddy and Whiskey gaps on the western end of the Ferris Mountains have also resulted from stream superimposition.

The Seminoe Mountains

The Seminoe Mountains, on the Continental Divide at the east rim of the Great Divide Basin, culminate in Bradley Peak (8,066'). They are primarily sedimentaries that have been uplifted with their granite cores dropped. They were named Seminole in 1877 by A.D. Wilson of the Hayden Survey, for Basil Cimineau Lajeunesse, one of Fremont's men, a French trapper and fur trader who established a trading post in 1858 on the Oregon Trail above Devils Gate. The Seminoes stretch east across the North Platte River where they are called the Bennett Mountains. Near their western border, the superimposed North Platte River had crossed the mountains from south to north, cutting a steep-walled canyon some 1,500' deep,

now known as Black Canyon. The Seminoes were thrust southward over Hanna Basin, an abrupt, very deep basin with a funnel-shaped downwarp. The contact point between granite and sedimentary rocks in the basin is 30,000' or more below that of those same rocks on the Seminoe Mountains surface to the north. It is the deepest downwarp in North America, deeper than Mount Everest is high. Its Cretaceous, Paleocene, and Eocene sedimentaries were folded into U's with seams of coal up to 50' thick tucked within the U's.

At the southeast corner of the Great Basin Divide, just west of Rawlins, is the Rawlins Uplift, a Laramide hump that didn't quite make it as a mountain. However, this small but sharply flexed uplift, with a Precambrian rock core and flanking hogbacks of Paleozoic rocks, is a veritable miniature Rocky Mountain structure within the Wyoming Basin. In a roadcut along I-80 just west of Rawlins, it reveals a 2,600-million-year time span. The Red Rim–China Butte area just south of Rawlins is critical winter range for the basin's 2,400 pronghorn. Their lives are bound to be affected by increased coal mining in the basin.

Eastern Outlier Ranges

The Pedro, Bennett, Shirley and Freezeout mountains, eastern outliers of the Granite Mountains, lie east of the North Platte and bound the Shirley Basin to the west and south. The granitic Pedros, east of the south end of Pathfinder Reservoir and north of the Bennetts, rise precipitously 2,000' from the desert to Pyramid Peak at 8,316'. Mostly BLM land, the Pedros provide winter roosting

Top: Bradley Peak is the only portion of the Seminoe Range on the Divide. Bottom: The true mustang, Spanish-blooded horses of the conquistadores, has long since disappeared. Today's mustangs, or "broomtails," are ranchers' stock gone wild.
RON MAMOT PHOTOS

areas for some 20 bald eagles, an ideal place for research and observation of eagle winter habitat. The Bennetts, east of Black Canyon and Seminoe Dam, and based by red cliff bands, chain east to the Shirley Mountains. The Shirleys, eastern stub end of the Seminoes, are anticlinal uplifts, folded sediments with no granite core, unique for this area. Madison limestone has formed prominent white hogbacks along the flanks that contain several caves and karst areas. Old hay meadows mark former homesteads of early Finlanders. The Freezeouts, eastern stub of the Granite Mountain Uplift, melt into the Laramie Range. The eastern Freezeouts contain striking examples of complexly folded and fractured sedimentary rocks that form sinuous, zig-zag or offset ridges and valleys—"race track" valleys or small closed topographic basins.

Oregon Buttes

The Continental Divide Trail heads south from South Pass to Continental Peak and Oregon Buttes, two erosional remnants of Eocene and Miocene sediments that rise precipitously 1,500' above the surrounding plain. This skyline jumble of stark hills, seen for many miles, were welcome landmarks for users of the Emigrant Trail and travelers on the South Pass Stage Road. Near these landmarks a Mormon handcart company of 500 people, led by James G. Willie, was caught in an 1856 blizzard; 100 people died. Preserved in the buttes' colorful sediments, deposited 40 million and then 20 million years ago, are fossils of primates, primitive rhinos, small three-toed horses, crocodiles and turtles, which indicate a tropical climate prevailed at the time of deposition.

The greater Wyoming Basin contains 38 Landmark Sites that the National Park Service studied in the 1970s. In the Great Divide Basin alone, BLM identified 10 Wilderness Study Areas surrounding and including the Killpecker sand dunes—a total of 186,279 acres, all with something noteworthy in special wildlife habitat, archaeological sites, geological wonders or ecological significance.

The Great Divide Basin is a vast dry oval whose rim, the Continental Divide, girdles a volcanic field, mountain ranges and sand dunes, and whose sunbaked floor hides a wealth of energy sources—coal, oil, gas, and uranium, now being developed. Curiously, precipitation falling here along the Continental Divide flows neither east nor west but sinks into the ground.

Above: Oregon Buttes signalled the Continental Divide for Oregon Trail travelers. It is the northern point where the Continental Divide splits into the Atlantic and Pacific rims of the "Divided Divide" that form the Great Divide Basin. LORRAINE G. BONNEY

Right: The rainbow colors of Honeycomb Buttes make this the most brilliant example of badlands in Wyoming. LORRAINE G. BONNEY

From South Pass the Continental Divide heads south through Continental Peak to Oregon Buttes, then splits around Great Divide Basin (locally, called the Red Desert), an area of interior drainage. The western or Pacific prong follows a low divide that passes east of Boar's Tusk, through Steamboat Mountain (8,683'), the Killpecker Dunes and the Leucite Hill. The eastern or Atlantic prong follows a higher divide through the Green, Ferris and Seminoe mountains and the Rawlins Uplift, both divides reuniting 89 miles to the south at Bridger Pass, with the single divide continuing south through the Sierra Madre Range into Colorado.

The Great Divide Basin, some 3,000 square miles or 2.25 million acres perched on top of the continent, contains shallow lakes that have no outlet. This country is really big and vulnerable—put a grader's blade down anywhere and you have an indelible road. Nevertheless, the sense of solitude here is an overwhelming experience. Planners should consider the area as an ecosystem regardless of existing boundaries. Ecologically it is still as it was a hundred years ago.

Continental Peak was included in BLM's Honeycomb Buttes Wilderness Study Area. Its 41,620 acres contain several terrain types, ranging from sagebrush hills and greasewood flats surrounding the Honeycomb badlands, to the eroding buttes with their many bluffs, small draws and side canyons. It is the best example of badland topography in Wyoming, with a rainbow of vivid colors—red, gray, white, yellow and violet bands. The many cliffs, ridges, draws and secluded grottos provide solitude. Many erosion caves provide a highly unusual experience in caving. Besides the more common antelope, deer, coyotes and raptors, there are mountain lions, spotted bats and wild horses. Fossilized turtle shell, agates, jade and petrified wood are found here.

Leucite Hills

The Leucite Hills area, once considered for the Registry of Natural Landmarks, include the Leucite Hills, nearby buttes and mesas, old volcanic necks, sand dunes, Steamboat Mountain and Black Rock. It is ecologically diverse and interesting because of the dunes, the isolated desert mountains, the seeps along the mountain sides, and the high abrupt cliffs that provide nesting sites for birds of prey such as the prairie falcon, golden eagle and red-tailed hawk.

The Leucite Hills, Boars Tusk and Black Rock are erosional remnants of a very young (Late Pliocene) volcanic field that form the western boundary of the Great Divide Basin. Once the Tertiary blanket was eroded away, these resistant lava-capped mesas were left standing some 600' above the surrounding area. Boars Tusk is a spectacular snag of a volcanic plug, a neck of volcanic material that solidified in a vent, from which the surrounding material eroded. Its spongy blackness has been limed by birds for generations. Black Rock and Pilot Butte are outliers of the same volcanic field. The Leucite Hills are of worldwide interest to geologists as the world's richest (first in North America) locality where the mineral leucite was reported, one of the most unusual rocks in mineral and chemical composition.

Steamboat Mountain, on the Continental Divide at 8,693', is a mountain rising out of the desert, truly an

The first ascent of Boars Tusk, a leucite monolith rising 200' above the surrounding talus cone, is unrecorded, but its three towers have been climbed many times. Where the breccia is solid, it has good bucketholds. RON MAMOT

oasis in the middle of the Red Desert. Of volcanic origin, Eocene plant fossils were found on the west face under a dateable basaltic flow. Some 119 plant species now grow here, including Douglas fir. Springs and seeps create very special microhabitats for such species as wild iris, blue-eyed grass and shooting stars. Two species of rodents are found on the mountain—yellow-bellied marmot and Wortman's golden-mantled ground squirrel. The Tri-Territorial Monument, near Steamboat Mountain, marks the intersection of the Louisiana Purchase, Oregon Territory and Texas Territory.

The 170-square-mile Killpecker Sand Dunes, one of the largest active dune fields in North America, is a mesmerizing geometry of ripples and hollows. It is unique in its combination of stable and unstable sand dunes with a diversity of wildlife—wild horses, mule deer, a rare (for here) herd of desert elk, many pronghorn antelope, raptors, coyotes, and even cougars.

The main dune belt funnels through an east-west gap in the Rock Springs Uplift, crosses the Continental Divide and Leucite Hills at 7,400', and extends 40 miles into the Great Divide Basin. The dunes reflect climatic fluctuations in the Wind River Range since the Ice Age. They've been occupied by humans for at least 111,000 years, as attested by nearby Eden Valley. Artifacts are constantly being found as the dunes move. Man must have watched the demise of the glaciers as a mixed blessing. The warming climate made life easier but the area also became drier. As aridity increased, the once-heavy mantle of vegetation died; large areas of bare soil became exposed to the elements. Winds swept across carrying grains of sand from the basin deposits, funneling toward the few low spots in the barrier; thus the dunes began.

The Bureau of Land Management owns some 60,800 acres of roadless-area dunes, which it divided into four Wilderness Study Areas, none of which was approved for wilderness status. In addition to the outstanding features mentioned, its most unusual feature is the collection of Eolian ice-cells that feed pools at the bases of many large dunes. Formed as snow and ice that collect on the lee side of the dunes, they are covered by blowing sand. These pools range in depth from 6" to 8' deep, some being crystal clear and almost sterile, while others are muddy and teeming with tadpoles and other small life, waterfowl, grasses and algae. Rock Spring residents have a

The Killpecker Dunes (above and right), whose constantly shifting sand dunes creep closer to abandoned buildings. LORRAINE G. BONNEY PHOTOS

dune buggy paradise in their backyard, but the machines are being confined to certain areas by the BLM in order to save some of the dunes.

Killpecker is a strange name, and it does have historical significance. It is related to the naming of Wamsutter, a town built with the Union Pacific Railroad, where the fellows were having health problems as a result of contact with the women who worked the line. The good doctor in town would take care of the "working girls" who nicknamed him the "womb setter," which developed into Wamsutter. The name Killpecker was a byproduct of the situation.

North of the Granite Mountain Uplift is a very different picture. After travelling westward on U.S. Highway 287 for many miles across the rolling sagebrush-grasslands of the Sweetwater Plateau, catching sight of the Beaver Divide or Rim southeast of Lander provides an abrupt and spectacular change in scenery and an equally great change in flora and fauna. The view as one descends from the high Beaver Rim scarp into Wind River Basin via U.S. Highway 287 is breathtaking—a panoramic sweep over the basin toward the Wind River Range. The rim is a drainage divide separating the Sweetwater River system, on the south, from several northerly flowing intermittent streams on the north.

Geologically, Beaver Rim was a "missing link" discovery, the first find of a neatly laid-out section of continuous Tertiary from Early Eocene through Miocene epochs. Fossil fragments collected by a local ranchman directed the attention of an amateur collector, N.H. Brown, to this escarpment, where he was totally surprised to find a rhinoceros skull. This led to many professional expeditions to the Rim, including those by the American Museum of Natural History in 1909 and 1910.

In addition, Beaver Rim illustrates the vast difference between the level of the Miocene basin fill and the level of erosion on the present basin floor. It also shows a good case of headward erosion and stream capture. Back in Pleistocene time, an upwarp at the south end of Wind River Basin diverted the Wind River northward and steepened its gradient over that of the mellower Sweetwater drainage. In this way, the vigorous Wind River tributaries developed the Beaver Divide by headward erosion. From the top of the windswept rim down to its sagebrush-grassland base there is a diversity of habitats on its escarpments.

The Rattlesnake Hills

The Wyoming Basin provided its own local volcanic area in the Rattlesnake Hills, which are east of the Beaver Divide. The Rattlesnakes are a low, isolated, narrow range of hills, the young erosional remnants of a swarm of some 42 Tertiary volcanic vents that opened just north of the Granite Mountains Uplift, blowing straight out through the Precambrian basement alkalic rocks and quite distinct from the volcanics of the Absaroka-Yellowstone area. The influence of this volcanic field was local, confined to an area within 30 miles of the vents. The crests of these volcanic plugs, like Garfield Peak (8,210'), are higher than the surrounding region because of the sunken Granite Mountains to the south. Abundant mass movement— slumps, rockfall, earth and mud flows— show that the earth is still on the move here.

North of Beaver Divide sit the Gas Hills, uranium mining center. Several miles north of the Gas Hills is the Love Ranch, close to the geographical center of Wyoming, where Dr. Dave Love, Wyoming's noted geologist, was born in 1913.

Devils Playground. Surrounding Black Mountain and Twin Buttes is this Wilderness Study Area, a highly eroded badlands devoid of vegetation except for the high outcrops where patches of juniper and sparse grasses survive.
BUREAU OF LAND MANAGEMENT

YELLOWSTONE-ABSAROKA VOLCANICS

Castle Geyser, miniature portrait of the history of Yellowstone, the hotspot that wouldn't go away.
PAT O'HARA

The Firehole River and Midway Geyser Basin, where the earth's crust is a mere two to six miles thick. PAT O'HARA

The nation's first national park, Yellowstone National Park was created in 1872 because of its wonders as an active volcanic hotspot. Actually there were at least two major volcanic episodes, one centered in the Absarokas and the more recent Yellowstone caldera event. The former was during early Cenozoic time when andesitic lavas spread from a landscape pockmarked by large strato-volcanoes similar to those of the present west coast of North America. In addition to the andesitic lava, steaming mudflows also spread from these volcanic cones, flowed down into the adjacent heavily forested valleys and buried the trees, thus petrifying them through the past 50 million years.

The craters, or more properly calderas, came into existence in Yellowstone only about 2 million years ago (early Quaternary time). They were characterized by fiery clouds of ash that erupted along ring-shaped fractures at the edges of the 40-mile-wide bulge that ultimately became a collapsed caldera itself. The ash welded into a resistant rock (welded tuff) that spread in all directions over the landscape away from the caldera. In addition to this airborne material, frequent rhyolite and some basalt lava flows were developed in conjunction with "resurgence" of the caldera, covering much of Yellowstone Plateau. The caldera complex erupted in three principal episodes, each 600,000 years apart, the latest being about 600,000 years before the present.

This explosive area already has proven itself 30 times more explosive than Krakatoa (1883) or Tambora (1815). Mt. St. Helens (1980) was a firecracker in comparison. At least three times it demolished up to a third of the current park in titanic explosions.

Yellowstone National Park is perched on a high plateau made up of three parts—Precambrian basement rocks created more than 2 billion years ago, then vertically uplifted; the dark-colored Absaroka volcanics that were erupted 52 to 32 million years ago; the light-colored Yellowstone volcanic rocks of the last 2 million years.

Up until 50 million years ago Yellowstone went through the same throes of landscaping that built up the rest of Wyoming's mountains. By the end of the Laramide Orogeny, northern Yellowstone had arched into a broad anticline, its Precambrian core thrust southwest, and its Paleozoic and Mesozoic sedimentaries crumpled, torn and faulted into several decent-size ranges (the Gallatin for

Ramshorn Peak in the Absarokas.
JEFF & PAT VANUGA

Mt. Washburn forms the north rim of the great Yellowstone Caldera.
PAT O'HARA

one), in and around the area. Several small anticlines in south Yellowstone were gently heaved up. Then came a savage time.

Fifty-two million years ago, darkish lava surged by the cubic mile from vents along the western edge of the Beartooth Plateau—the start of the Absaroka Range. It buried the landscape under 3,000' of Stygian debris and built up large, steep-sided stratovolcanoes of layered lava, breccia and volcanic ash.

One of these, the Sherman volcano, burst forth at the northeast corner of today's park in early Tertiary times and buried the country under 2,000' of lava. Mt. Washburn (10,243') is a remnant of one old volcano that centered to the south, perhaps near the Washburn Hot Springs; Bunsen Peak was an equally important volcanic center. The Gallatin Range was covered and engulfed along its crest (then a lowland) by 6,000 feet of breccia, or mudflows, and andesitic lava from a host of volcanoes both in Yellowstone and in the Gallatin Range itself. To the east, lava engulfed a forest, then banked up a-

Petrified trees on Specimen Ridge.
MICHAEL FRANCIS

gainst the west flanks of the Absaroka Range, and to the south it buried the outlying spurs of the Tetons and Wind River Range.

The Oligocene and Miocene years were comparatively quiet as the Rockies—defeated by erosion—were buried in their own debris and that of the volcanoes, which belched out such enormous amounts that an ashy desert smothered what would be Wyoming and buried the mountain ranges up to their chins. Pliocene time brought the general arching that boosted the Rockies and Yellowstone-Absaroka plateaus a mile above sea level. This stretched the crust, breaking it into blocks—some of which rose while others sank. Pliocene volcanoes poured out viscous, frothy, pinkish-gray and brown lava called rhyolite that engulfed the northern end of the Tetons.

A little more than 2 million years ago, magma collected in a huge blisterlike cavern directly below the center of Yellowstone. Under great gas pressure, it poked, prodded and tested the crust above, bulging it, rupturing it here and there so that small amounts of magma escaped through fractures. As more magma escaped, the pressure eased, giving the heated gases room to expand—which they did, with a vengeance. They burst through the ring of fractures with herculean force, belching hot rock, froth and ash into the sky. In one indescribably ferocious moment, the Absaroka volcanoes and one third of modern Yellowstone were destroyed. Dust and debris billowed into the air, blotting out the sun, turning day into night. The expanding gas shot clouds of ash flows down the conic slopes, where they turned into rock. More than 600 cubic miles of volcanic debris drenched the country, as far away as Saskatchewan and Texas, with yellow Huckleberry Ridge Tuff. Once spent, the great chamber collapsed into its crater.

It all happened again 1.2 million years ago in Island Park, but the extravagant fireworks held off until 600,000 years ago when, on a scale known nowhere else in recorded geologic history, and with an explosive force many times more vicious and far-reaching than Mt. St. Helens, the lid was blown off the great magma chamber. Magma had been churning upward into underground chambers, bulging the surface into a dome-like mountain 50 to 75 miles across. As surface crust split and fractured, lava leaked out. Preliminary rumbles and smoking climaxed in a massive explosion as huge avalanches of hot gas erupted. The hot cloud of Lava Creek ash mushroomed 600 cubic

miles of debris in all directions and blacked out the sun, perhaps for years. Some of the spreading ash cloud, hot and inflated with gas, flowed like water, then stopped and collapsed, forming a tuff a hundred feet thick. Some of the ash caught the winds and, flying too high to weld, covered half today's United States in ash. It blanketed Wyoming in a thick unconsolidated layer that is now gone except for a few rare spots. On the Continental Divide near I-80 in southern Wyoming, more than 200 miles from its source, a 30- to 40-acre patch of bright white Lava Creek ash, 60 feet thick, still can be seen.

The panoramic view from Mt. Washburn takes in much of the Yellowstone caldera, the colossal volcanic collapse complex from 600,000 years ago. Not completely suspecting its fiery origin, Dr. F.V. Hayden first noticed it in 1871 from the top of Mt. Washburn: "...a bird's-eye view of the entire basin may be obtained, with the mountains surrounding it on every side without any apparent break in the rim. This basin has been called by some travelers the vast crater of an ancient volcano." Its 50-mile-wide rim is nearly the largest in the world. Mt. Washburn is a remnant of its north rim. Mt. Sheridan (10,308'), west of Heart Lake, the Red Mountains and Flat Mountain also were parts of its rim; the Absarokas were its eastern rim. The Washburn Range and cliffs north of Madison Junction form other sections of the crater rim.

Yellowstone Lake formed when rainwater, snowmelt and rivers were trapped in the partly downwarped depression remaining from the caldera. The lake's waters spilled over the edge as the lower Yellowstone River, which cut through the rolling lava plateau to form the Grand Canyon of the Yellowstone. Fumaroles and hot springs throughout the Canyon area have, for centuries, chemically altered the brown and gray rhyolite canyon walls into the rich yellows and oranges—yellow stone! The tempestuous past of the park is told in the walls of the Grand Canyon of the Yellowstone, which show seven layers of relatively recently petrified forests in its rocks. The lava surface cooled, but heat held deep in its base over hundreds of thousands of years still spouts the geysers and steams the hot pools of the Yellowstone. The "frozen" standing forest of Specimen Ridge is the ancient visible remains of a deciduous southern forest that grew at the 2,000' level 55 million years ago. It was completely and rapidly engulfed by broken-up lava and ash carried in steamy mud off the flanks of the relatively active volcanoes of this area, 50 million years ago. Thus buried, the trees absorbed silica from the ash and mud, and were preserved. The 27 layers found here show that between each of the volcanic cycles forests grew in the new volcanic soil only to be destroyed by the next series of volcanic outbursts. Lesser blasts buried—and so preserved—nearby trees under clouds of ash, dust and other debris, creating Yellowstone's 40 square miles of fossil forest, the world's largest.

The Gallatin Range, of 10,000' granite and volcanic breccia, extends into the northwest corner of Yellowstone Park, culminating in Electric Peak (10,992'), so named because Henry Gannett of the Hayden Survey climbed it in 1872 during a storm and suffered from what he noted as "extraordinary" electrical phenomena.

The Red Mountains

The Red Mountains, a small isolated range topped by Mt. Sheridan (10,308'), rise above the volcanic plateau of southern Yellowstone, adjacent to Heart Lake. The area is important habitat, heavily used by grizzlies and by a large elk herd in summer. From the road near Lewis Lake, the Red Mountains look like a high forested range of hills, but in them, particularly on the eastern slopes, there is an un-expected diversity including cirque basins with little lakes, and matchless vistas. In his 1876 Snake River journal, Lt. G. C. Doane described Mt. Sheridan as "...the youngest of the mountains in that region. Its lava flows are on the surface everywhere...It is a fragment of an old cra-ter rounded off by frost action into a quite regular cone... Its slopes are mostly bare and of dull reddish yellow col-or. It apparently needs only to be kindled well in order to burst forth in lava flows again." A steep switchbacked trail leads to a windswept knife-edge ridge that looks its part as the rim of the Yellowstone Caldera.

On "the night the mountain fell," in 1959, an earthquake that was centered at Montana's Hebgen Lake, just west of Yellowstone, registered 7.5 on the Richter scale. It was the strongest quake on record in the Rocky Mountains and the second strongest in the history of North America. The U.S. Geological Survey rushed teams into Yellowstone to find out what had happened, followed later by NASA (to test remote-sensing equipment) and geologists from the University of Utah (for seismic studies). They found Yellowstone was rimmed by the tectonically most active mountains in the northern Rockies; that a huge reservoir

Above: Heart Lake and Mt. Sheridan, south rim of the Caldera, from Hancock Peak. HOWIE WOLKE

Left: Electric Peak in the Gallatin Range. GEORGE WUERTHNER

73

Doane and Stephenson Peaks in the Absaroka Range, Yellowstone National Park. MICHAEL H. FRANCIS

of superheated molten rock lay under Yellowstone, keeping the geysers hot; that Yellowstone was one great interconnected hot-water system; that the caldera erupted in 600,000-year intervals; that the floor of Yellowstone was doming, meaning enormous pressures were building up underground, perhaps the first stage of a new volcanic cycle; that the earth's crust averaged 25 miles thick but in Yellowstone it was only two to six miles thick.

The Yellowstone area is under siege again, not from volcanoes at the moment, but from plans! Yellowstone Park stands at the center of a national treasure, the largest remaining intact ecosystem in the temperate zones of the earth—the Greater Yellowstone Ecosystem.

The Absaroka Range

The Absarokas: Wyoming's mysterious, least known and most misunderstood range of mountains. The Absarokas: a vast confusion of crumbly snowy peaks, deep canyons, disoriented streams and haunting tales. The Absarokas: homeland of moose, elk, cougar, marten and bighorn sheep; where the grizzly seeks elbow room in one of its last refuges; where barely accessible places provided a last refuge for the ancient stone-culture Sheepeaters.

Even the name adds to the mystique. The area once was part of the country of the Crow or Absaroka Indians,

whose name has been pronounced Absaro'ka, Absor'ka or Absor'kee (in Montana). Hodge, in *Handbook of the American Indian,* says Absa'roka, meaning "people of the great winged bird."

How is it that this vast mountain wilderness called the Absarokas can still be described, in the words of Aldo Leopold, as "a blank spot on the map" even though it is as well-mapped as the rest of Wyoming?

It is because this awesome region is perhaps the least known, the least understood, and certainly the least appreciated mountain area in the state. This spectacular range was conventionally uplifted in conjunction with Montana's Beartooth Mountains in Laramide times, some 50 to 30 million years ago, its broad, rugged crest stretching southward from Montana for more than 80 miles to connect with the Wind River Range at Togwotee Pass. As Yellowstone's east boundary, and containing the headwaters of the Yellowstone, Shoshone, Greybull, and Wood rivers, the Absarokas rise in a bold unbroken barrier of rough country dominated by 11,000' and 12,000' peaks with Francs Peak, at 13,153', the highest in the Rockies north of the Wind River Range.

As Yellowstone is the heart, the Absaroka Range is the torso of the Greater Yellowstone Ecosystem, with its four large wilderness areas—the Washakie, North and South Absaroka and Teton. All this, plus Yellowstone and Grand Teton parks, forms the largest (6,600 square miles) and one of the most rugged, wildest, and untouched wilderness complexes and premier habitats of the Lower 48.

The Absaroka Range is a colossal pile of volcanic lava and breccia laid down in "layer cake" fashion and never extensively folded. The range's underpinnings, though, consist of folded and faulted older rocks. Born of the spewings from thousands of fissures that poured out lava by the cubic mile, the Absarokas' plateau-like crest coincides with the top of a vast, nearly horizontal blanket of lava, cinders and ash that was blasted from a great chain of tremendously active volcanoes—Francs Peak, Younts Peak, the Yellowstone caldera—debris that covered most of northwest Wyoming.

These mountains, trimmed to size by erosion, are a classic example of erosion development—the deep dissection of relatively flat-lying rock layers. Laid down mostly in Tertiary times, the strata are primarily fragments of andesitic lava, which characterized the area's volcanoes of 50 million years ago. The Absaroka breccias spread over the entire area of present Yellowstone Park, and the Gallatin Range to the northwest, as well as over the entire Absaroka Range. Streams cut into this plateau in every which way and direction, followed by the carving action of glaciers, leaving narrow steeply-walled canyons, some of them 2,000 to 5,000 feet in depth, rising to a complex of unorganized divides and isolated sloping plateau remnants.

One of the unique climactic actions of the Absarokas can be seen on the 1985 USGS Geological Map of Wyoming. Zeroing in on the Absarokas brings you right to the dazzling center of a radiating dike field, the Sunlight Intrusives, where tiny red lines, the intrusives, radiate outward in a glorious sunburst about four inches in diameter. This is one of the most spectacular such formations in the Rockies. Picture a tube-like sponge cake with the hole blocked at the top, then imagine a cake decorator full of icing, forcing icing up into the hole from below. So it was with this volcanic center. The andesitic lava was jetted forcefully up from the center into the surrounding fractured rocks—result: hundreds of dikes of intruded molten rock radiating from the center. But unlike the Yellowstone caldera, it didn't collapse on itself or blow itself apart, but held its intriguing shape.

The Absarokas are characterized by steep slopes, startling pinnacles, colorful banded cliffs, hidden narrow canyons, swift clear streams, broad grassy ridge tops above timberline. Weird caricature shapes and bizarre sculptures, called "hoodoos," have been eroded in the weathered stone, all adding to the mystique and legends. Many Indians shunned the range, believing it to be haunted with little cliff-dwelling people who tossed rocks down, or because mountain sides that smoldered with fires burned one's feet. For the inquisitive explorer, the recesses of this last true wilderness preserve numerous puzzles, such as, did the great rock arrow built on a high ridge above Sunlight Creek and pointing eastward have a significant link to the mysterious Medicine Wheel in the Bighorn Range 85 miles to the northeast?

It's a surprise to see broad rolling uplands above timberline (11,000' to 12,000') that recall the moors of Scotland, or, around the corner, petrified giants of a past forest. The view across a landscape of bogs, small lakes and numerous small streams and stratified peaks gives no sense of height and mountain character until one looks in-

Breccia Peak above Brooks Lake. Gros Ventre Range is in the background. WILLIAM B. HALL

to the plunging depths of a major valley. The unexpected vertical relief takes the breath away. Surprises come in the eruption, not of volcanos, but of spectacular fields of wildflowers of every color in this acidic, potassium-rich soil. The few determined botanists who scout its plateaus have discovered several species of mustard native to Alaska in patches of true Alaska-style permafrost. Two new species unknown elsewhere in the world also have been found. Inaccessibility has helped to preserve surprises such as a 300-year-old stands of virgin spruce and whitebark pine.

In the Absarokas, one can experience the unexpected discovery of parallel rows of rocks piled five feet apart near the edge of a steep cliff; or flakes of smoky gray or black obsidian; or a tepee ring of stone 14 feet in diameter, the few remnant clues left by the ancient Sheepeaters, or Tukuarika, who flitted in and out of the accounts of early western travelers. A. Hultkrantz, in *The Shoshones in the Rocky Mountains,* called them peaceful

and harmless, timid and wary. They spoke the Shoshonean language, lived in small family or related groups, traveled on foot, and used their large dogs for hunting, as pack animals, or to drag the loaded V-shaped travois. They lived off the land, fishing as they went, moving with the harvest, gathering berries, herbs and plants from late spring to early fall. The Englishman, William Baillie-Grohman, traveling in the Wind River Range in 1880, frequently came across their lodges which, he said, were "without exception the most miserable human dwellings I ever saw...consisting of loosely piled-up stones, and lean-to roof of slender pine trunks...found 800 or 1000 feet over Timberline." Captain B.L.E. Bonneville, in 1833, described them as "a kind of hermit race, scanty in number, that inhabit the highest and most inaccessible vastness...They are miserably poor, own no horses, and carry their provisions, clothing, skins, etc., on dogs...Their weapons are bows and stone-pointed arrows, with which they hunt the deer, the elk, and the mountain sheep."

In this great wilderness there are still glaciers—the Sunlight Peak Glacier, the great Fishhawk Glacier, the DuNoir Glacier, the little known Borron Creek Glacier—standing petrified trees, several natural bridges, many permanent snowfields, and several caves. At the Mummy Cave, actually a rock shelter 34 miles west of Cody along the Cody-Yellowstone highway, a 1,300-year-old mummified Indian was found, along with artifacts preserved by the extremely dry climate of the cave. Excavated by the Whitney Gallery of Western Art in Cody, the cave proved a very rich early-man site, continuously used by Indians from 7280 B.C. to about 1800 A.D. The artifacts, on view in the Cody gallery, covered 38 culture layers and threw new light on the prehistoric cultures of the Rocky Mountain region.

Continuing studies in the Teton, Yellowstone and Absaroka areas have turned up more evidence that Paleo man appeared while the last ice age still lingered, some 9,000 years ago. Datable obsidian points, butchering tools, stone fire rings and roasting ovens containing charred camas roots indicate some of the activities these early inhabitants enjoyed.

Knowledge of the Absarokas was first carried back by John Colter who, with his two buddies, Forrest Hancock and Joseph D. Dickson, had a taste of its wildness in 1806 when they spent some time huddled in a lean-to built in the recess of a cliff in Sunlight Basin. Early-day trapper

Facing page: Pinnacles in the Absarokas. JEFF VANUGA
Top: Lower Sunlight Basin from Dead Indian Pass.
LORRAINE G. BONNEY
Bottom: Jules Bowl above Brooks Lake. GEORGE WUERTHNER

Osborne Russell made one of the first climbs in the range in 1837 when he ascended what he called "the highest mountain" of a cirque, reaching the snow in an hour of foot travel somewhere in the northeast corner of Yellowstone Park. However, most trappers avoided the 80-mile barrier of rough terrain since there were few beaver and little gold to attract them. The survey groups were the next to probe the edges. Eventually the rugged isolated range became the ideal hideout for horse thieves like Joe Bliss, who was killed by a posse in 1892 in today's Bliss Creek Meadow.

The story of Harry S. Yount, "Rocky Mountain Harry," is nearly lost in legend even though his name was given to the highest peak in the Teton Wilderness, Younts Peak (12,165'), source of the Yellowstone River. Yount was a scout and packer for the 1878 Hayden survey (he climbed West Spur of the Grand Teton with the survey that year). In June 1800 he was hired as Lamar Valley gamekeeper by P.W. Norris, Yellowstone superintendent. Norris, appalled by the wanton slaughter of game in the park, proposed saving the remaining bands of animals by turning the northeast corner of the park into a game preserve. Yount, as gamekeeper (and thereby the first national park "ranger") lived in the cabin built for him in the angle between Soda Butte Creek and the upper Lamar River. It only needed one solitary winter among the herds for him to realize that one man was useless, and he told Norris that "a small and reliable police force of men..." was really needed. Yount had come to Wyoming in 1866. As hunter, trapper and guide, he killed 57 grizzly bears, was tracked by Indians and knew chiefs Red Cloud, Spotted Tail and Dull Knife. He hunted buffalo for food but never participated in decimation of the herds. He hunted various animal specimens for the Smithsonian Institution, and was known as a voracious reader during his solitary hunting and trapping years. He died in Wheatland in 1924.

The nation's first national forest was established by President Harrison as The Yellowstone Park Timberland Reserve on March 30, 1891, now part of the Shoshone National Forest. Wapiti Ranger Station on the Cody-Yel-

The west DuNoir, named by early French explorers for its luxuriant black timber. HOWIE WOLKE

lowstone highway is the oldest one in the United States.

Linking the Absaroka Range to the Wind River Range is the superb scenic beauty of the Continental Divide summits where U.S. Highway 287 crosses Togwotee Pass at the divide. To the east are the Shoshone National Forest,

Dubois, and the Wind River Basin; to the west is the magnificent descent route through Bridger-Teton National Forest to Moran and Jackson Hole, with the Tetons filling the western horizon. The pass lies in open meadows and pine forests but just north of the road is the impressive rampart of volcanic rocks known as Pinnacle Buttes. It lifts 1,364 above the pass to Breccia Peak (10,908'). Its bare walls expose stratified volcanic conglomerates striped with white bands of volcanic ash, which expose a complete sequence of some 65 million years of sedimentation. More importantly and less known, the sequence of vertebrate faunas recovered here is unparalleled. Erosion is causing the escarpment, the southern end of the Absaroka Range, to slowly migrate northward. The Togwotee Pass area sits above the buried Washakie Range.

Holmes Cave, northwest of Togwotee Pass in Teton Wilderness, was discovered in 1898 by E. B. Holmes who mapped the two-level passage in 1905. The map is in the Jackson Hole Historical Museum in Jackson. Near the cave entrance, a large sink hole, there was found some 50-million-year-old tropical swamp debris. Crater Lake to the north could be the result of the collapse of buried karst under the surface volcanic rocks. Enos Lake is in an area of shattered chaotic limestone, which could have collapsed and formed the lake.

For more than 20 years the magnificent DuNoir area east of Togwotee Pass has been held in suspension as a Special Management Area of the Shoshone National Forest, a compromise designation created for it in the 1960s to save its virginal forest. The Forest Service strenuously opposed its inclusion in the Washakie Wilderness.

Ever since the first French explorers crossed the Absarokas into the head of the twin DuNoir drainages and named them for their luxuriant black timber, the lumbering potential of the area has been obvious. Just as obvious was its wilderness potential as discovered by Orrin Bonney and his group of Sierra Clubbers who were studying wilderness boundaries for hearings coming up in the '60s. They had just discovered the government-managed timber depredation of the beautiful Jules Bowl near Togwotee Pass, and in the DuNoir found the timber interests gnawing around the edges of the Wolf Creek virgin-like forest. Bonney's group headed for Dubois where they alerted Joe and Mary Back and the entire Dubois citizenry about what was going on.

Shoshone National Forest officials were dead set against a DuNoir wilderness area, although it was bounded by both the Washakie and Teton wildernesses, and was a contiguous corner of the Yellowstone ecosystem. Over the strenuous objections of the Forest Service and the timber industry, Congress, with the help of Congressman Teno

Roncalio, decreed 28,000 acres of the DuNoir as a Special Management Area because Roncalio believed that "...the entire DuNoir basin was not only eligible for inclusion as wilderness, but was, in fact, probably the most desirable area in all of Wyoming to be wilderness."

Like most of this country, the DuNoir was logged long ago by the Scandanavian 'tie hacks' who took the best trees, cutting by hand half a million railroad ties from the Engelmann spruce, subalpine and Douglas fir, and whitebark and lodgepole pine. The ties were cut to exact size on site and stored behind small log retention dams. With spring floods, the dams were dynamited and the ties floated down to the Wind River and thence to Riverton. Rotting cabins, blown log-dams, a few stumps were all that remained in the forests around the DuNoir meadows from that historically rich era, minor detractions from its wilderness quality. As one of the last protected drainages of the upper Wind River, it is an important summer range and migration corridor for wildlife. It supports a resident herd of 350 elk, but more important, it serves as a migration route and calving ground for more than a thousand elk on the east side of the Continental Divide. Should the DuNoir be clearcut, Game and Fish officials believe that the elk wintering east of the divide will be steered into the already-full wintering areas west of the divide. The DuNoir is home for moose, bighorn sheep, mule deer, black bear, grizzlies and trumpeter swans.

The latest skirmish over the DuNoir came in 1984 with the passing of the Wyoming Wilderness Act. Protagonists this time were a united Wyoming congressional delegation versus Rep. John Seiberling (D-Ohio), chairman of the House Interior Subcommittee on Public Lands. The state's trio in Washington favored a bill protecting 11,000 acres as wilderness but releasing the remaining 17,000 acres. Rep. Seiberling favored Wilderness status for the entire 28,000-acre Special Management Unit plus an additional 6,000 acres of the DuNoir. The deadlock resulted in no change in the area's status. So the DuNoir continues as a Special Management Area, a precarious category, to say the least.

The Washakie Range

Nobody suspected that the southern margin of the Absaroka Range (north of Dubois/U.S. Highway 287) wasn't what it appeared to be until young Wyoming geologist Dave Love, then a graduate student, picked that area for his Ph.D. thesis in the 1930s. Geologically, it was a

Cathedral Peak on Horse Creek, Washakie Wilderness. HOWIE WOLKE

Cub Creek in the Teton Wilderness.
HOWIE WOLKE

humed, either from a late start or because it was buried so deep. It is very hard to pin down on any map other than the USGS Geological Map of Wyoming, because it is topographically indistinct from its overshadowing Absaroka neighbor. Since it was buried by the southern Absarokas, traces of it show up along the south fringes of that range in a long arc westwards that starts at the low divide just west of the Owl Creek Range. The Washakies skirt westerly between the Absarokas and U.S. Highway 287, through Togwotee Pass and down toward Jackson Hole about ten miles, then head north through the middle of the Teton Wilderness ending at South Arm of Yellowstone Lake. The range is buried under some well known peaks—Washakie Needles, County Peak, the Ramshorn, Pinnacle Buttes, Terrace Mountain. It is west of Two Ocean Pass and Enos Lake is in the middle of it. At the mouth of the South Fork Buffalo, a western boundary of the Washakie Range, the 3,000' South Fork Canyon is a good place to see the core of the Washakie range with the Absaroka layers on top.

From a wilderness standpoint the Absaroka-Washakie ranges are a national treasure equal to anything in the Lower 48. This is home to the grizzly. Unfortunately, the important winter range for game, some 100,000 acres contiguous to the area, is found outside wilderness boundaries on the eastern drainages sloping into the Big Horn Basin. The Wyoming delegation's Wilderness Bill of 1984, a classic rock and ice proposal protecting high rocky pinnacles and glaciers, country of no use to commercial interests, opens up rich meadow and forest land for development.

The Absaroka-Washakie is subdivided into two main regions. The North Absaroka complex includes the North Absaroka Wilderness, adjacent roadless areas on the Shoshone National Forest, and a large roadless piece of northeastern Yellowstone National Park, making a large roadless area of some 900,000 acres in one tract. It's a neat, simple classic wilderness, along a distinct classic crest, the eastern boundary of Yellowstone Park. The water west of the border goes into the Lamar Creek/Yellowstone River drainage; everything east goes into the Shoshone River drainage, then up into the Yellowstone.

The larger South Absaroka complex, south of the Cody-Yellowstone highway, is big—2 million acres, including Teton Wilderness, Washakie Wilderness, the southeast corner of Yellowstone Park, and large contiguous road-

black hole. After some detective work, some exhuming and a lot of exploring and hiking, he discovered a jackpot—a set of buried mountain ranges on top of one another. Think of it! An entire chain of genetically different mountains largely buried under the Absaroka's pyroclastic pile. He named it the Washakie Range. He also found the west end of the Owl Creek Mountains likewise buried. He could see that the Absarokas were structurally different from the folded granite-cored Owl Creeks, but it took more work to discern that the Owls were younger than the Washakies and that the buried Washakies were folded, granite-cored, and had been thrust southwestward over the Wind River Basin.

The Washakie Range is still in the process of being ex-

less areas on both the Bridger-Teton and Shoshone national forests. Because it is managed in so many different administrative units, it doesn't receive the recognition of other big wildernesses, such as Montana's Bob Marshall Wilderness or Idaho's River of No Return. Geographically, it is an unorganized muddle of divides and drainages. Even the Continental Divide is whimsical; it follows the high Absaroka crest from Togwotee Pass northeast as the east boundary of Teton Wilderness for some 30 miles, then splits, bisecting the Teton Wilderness by taking the "low road" northwest across the Thorofare country into Yellowstone Park. The west side of the Absarokas is much wetter, with more precipitation as winter snow; the east side has more of a continental climate. Rivers in the South Absaroka Wilderness include some of the most important headwaters of both the

Left: The Washakie Range.
HOWIE WOLKE
Top: Owl Creek cabin and Washakie Needle. BUREAU OF LAND MANAGEMENT
Bottom: The Absarokas' stone arrow points northeast to the Medicine Wheel in the Bighorns. RON MAMOT

81

statues in niches of high walls, waiting for the forces of erosion to crash them down to the valley floor. Beautiful agatized wood, tree limbs, resin, and pine cones are the treasures disgracefully pirated by the packload as amateur and professional rockhounds swarm out of the Petrified Forest with packhorses illegally loaded with the loot. The folded Precambrian crystalline rocks of the ancestral Washakie Range are exposed within the (non-designated) Wiggins Fork Natural Landmark Area. The spectacular and vulnerable DuNoir Basin, Francs Peak and essential wildlife habitat and watersheds are under constant oil, gas and timber development threats, especially since the extremely oil-productive sediments of the Big Horn Basin can be identified under the Absarokas and maybe even over to Yellowstone's Grand Canyon where petroleum seeps out of the walls with hot water and steam.

The east-slope roadless areas, totally ignored by the Forest Service in RARE II, were recommended for non-wilderness. Their winter ranges for big game—Francs Peak, South Fork Shoshone, and Elk Fork of the North Fork—are extremely valuable for wildlife. The same uproar that occurred in Montana over oil and gas drilling plans on the Bob Marshall Wilderness should occur over developmental plans for the east slope of the Absarokas, but it won't happen. It is unfortunately adjacent to that part of Wyoming that is probably the most anti-wilderness part of the state, the Big Horn Basin. Or so it was thought until Marathon Oil tried to drill a well in a favored spot. Marathon proposed drilling a controversial well in the Wapiti Valley South Wilderness addition on Elk Fork, west of Cody, never thinking there would be opposition since it was next to Bighorn Basin territory. But a public outcry ensued; residents of Cody, including outfitters, were outraged because winter range, calving areas, grizzly habitat, were threatened. Marathon had to agree to do a helicopter exploration. Even then the people were opposed, but Marathon explored, came up dry and took the rig out.

Being snugged up against the southeast corner of Washakie Wilderness just east of Washakie Needles allows BLM's three tiny parcels (710 acres) of land to qualify as the Owl Creek Wilderness Study Area, a patchwork quilt of state, private and federal lands. Its major ridge line, rising to 10,900', divides the main drainages of South Fork Owl Creek, Rock Creek and South Fork of North Fork Owl Creek. This little niche is critical habitat to deer, elk, big horn sheep, raptors, small upland game animals, and

Top: Parting of the Waters at Two Ocean Pass. RON MAMOT *Above: Volcanic pinnacles above Wapiti Valley in North Fork Shoshone River canyon.* KENT & DONNA DANNEN *Facing page: Alpine wildflowers on the Beartooth Plateau.* JEFF GNASS

Columbia and Missouri River systems—with the east slope draining into the Yellowstone and the west side into the Snake—not the case of the North Absaroka which is east of the Continental Divide. There's a tremendous diversity from sagebrush grassland habitat at relatively low elevations along the eastern flank to moist Rocky Mountain forests along western slopes with alpine tundra and all the zones in between.

The 557,312-acre Teton Wilderness, at the southeast corner of Yellowstone, has an unspoiled natural grandeur including phenomena such as the Two Ocean Pass, South Buffalo Fork Falls, Big Springs on the Soda Fork, and North Fork Falls. At Two Ocean Pass, the "Parting of the Waters" is where Two Ocean Creek divides to become two creeks called Atlantic and Pacific creeks. One flows 3,488 miles into the Atlantic via Yellowstone, Missouri, and Mississippi rivers, while the other flows 1,353 miles into the Pacific via the Snake and Columbia. Its upper Thorofare country is world-class big-game habitat and outfitting is big business. Almost every large mammal indigenous to this part of the country still is here.

On the east side of the Absarokas, the Washakie Wilderness protects the spectacular rocky summits of the Washakie-Absaroka divide and the intriguing Petrified Forest, where petrified tree stumps stand like saintly possibly transient grizzlies. Its unexplored geology offers the study of tertiary volcanics.

This entire complex of magnificent wilderness and de facto wilderness is a shrinking resource. Although Wyoming's Wilderness Act of 1984 added the 40,000-acre Wyoming High Lakes and the 75,000-acre Deep Lake areas as wilderness study areas, it cut off 94,000 acres of essen-tial North Absaroka Wilderness additions.

Just north and northeast of Yellowstone Park is Montana's highest mountain range, the Beartooth Mountains, a broad domal Laramide uplift whose backside slopes gently down into Wyoming almost as a plateau. As the Beartooth uplifted and tilted south, Wyoming's tail-end piece was thrust eastward on to the Bighorn Basin, and most of the sediments on the Beartooth Plateau were dumped into Wyoming. These mountains are similar to the Washakie Range in that they have been overlapped by the uppermost part of the volcanic pile that comprises the Absaroka Range. South of the Red Lodge-Cooke City highway (U.S. Highway 212) is Wyoming's portion of the Beartooth Plateau, 23,750 acres of which have been added to Montana's Absaroka-Beartooth Wilderness. The eastern portion, popular with snowmobilers, was made into the 14,700-acre High Lakes Wilderness Study Area and its wild future is in doubt. Typical of the forested high Beartooth plateau, its all granitic subalpine-to-alpine terrain, haven for mountain goats, is dotted with numerous scenic lakes and ponds like Night and Beauty lakes.

However, the Wyoming Wilderness Act neglected to include the 75,000-acre Deep Lake area with the spectacular lower Clarks Fork Canyon, which follows a fault line and separates the Beartooth from the Absaroka Range. This was a terrible loss—a wild area in excess of 100,000 acres that nobody really knew about. A major portion of the well known Clarks Fork Canyon, long-time candidate for Scenic River status, is in this roadless area. From the Red Lodge-Cooke City highway, the land drops into high subalpine Deep Lake. Ridge views from tundra-covered Lime Creek Plateau are down deep glacial troughs which break dramatically into rough escarpments that drop down to desert at the north end of Bighorn Basin—altogether a 7,000-foot drop with changing vegetation. The only peat beds in the continental United States are found here, underlain with permafrost. Mountain goats have been introduced here, extending the southern end of their modern-day range.

SOUTHEAST CORNER MOUNTAINS

Balanced exfoliated Sherman granite boulder in the Vedauwoos.
KENT & DONNA DANNEN

Libby Lake backdropped by the climbing heaven of the Snowy Range. The Diamond is directly above the little island. JEFF GNASS

The corner of Wyoming opposite the famous northwest corner, has its own geological delights. Geologically, the southeast corner has a "gangplank" and an unusual drainage system in the Laramie Range, classic 2-billion-year-old algae reefs in the Medicine Bow Range, and the onetime largest copper mine in the world, in the Sierra Madres.

Recreationally, there is exceptional climbing in the Snowy Range and Veedauwoo rocks, and there are prime hunting, fishing, hiking and camping. Easy access to rare, wild, alpine scenery can be had by car.

One can look at the Colorado Front Range as like the palm of one's right hand, with three fingers extending into the southeast corner of Wyoming. The long middle finger, direct continuation of the Front Range, is the Laramie Mountains. To the west, the Laramie Basin separates the Laramie from the Medicine Bow mountains on the west, and the pinky is the Sierra Madre Range. These three mountain ranges, in the Medicine Bow National Forest, are glacially-carved terrain of igneous, metamorphic and sedimentary rock. The broad spectrum of geologic features includes faults, shear zones, dips, synclines and anticlines. The diverse geology of the area results in the presence of important minerals.

The Laramie Range

The Laramie Range, the northernmost extension into Wyoming of the Colorado Front Range, is a granite-cored anticlinal uplift, one of the last of the Laramide Orogeny uplifts, with a steep eastern flank and gentle rock slope on the west. Surrounded by sagebrush plains, the rugged slopes of this range are timbered almost to their summits with alpine Douglas fir, limber pine and some rare virgin ponderosa pine. Beautiful mountain parks and deep valleys lie between the rugged breaks. High, rocky, sharp peaks, and high narrow ridges covered with large boulders, characterize the range. A number of other peaks rise above 9,000', including Eagle and Blue Jay peaks.

This low-profiled, asymmetric mountain range has a unique drainage system. Conventional north-south ranges elsewhere are symmetrical, with west-side drainages draining to the west and east-side drainages flowing east. Here, most of the drainages flow across the entire range from west to east, paying no attention to the mountains. Breaking all rules of mountain construction, they

started in the high valley of the west-side Laramie Basin, following an established course inherited from an earlier master drainage on the high-level Tertiary sedimentary fill that had buried the mountains. As the basins were excavated on both sides of the range, the superimposed drainages kept pace, eroding down through the granite core of the range.

Shaped like a dogleg, the Laramie Range, first called "Black Hills," then named for trapper-explorer Jacques de la Ramie, starts near Casper at Casper Mountain, the northwest extremity of the range. It was thrust northward out onto younger sedimentary rocks, while the main part of the Laramies was thrust eastward out on the High Plains strata. Casper Mountain, the local ski area, is a rolling upland that rises more than 3,000' above the valley. Its north face is a precipitous fault scarp. From Casper Mountain the "black hills" silhouette of the Laramie Range rises ruggedly to Laramie Peak (10,274'), highest point east of the Rockies, then sagging down to the low relief at Interstate 80 at the "Gangplank."

The Gangplank is a narrow strip of Tertiary rocks that

Top: Vedauwoo Rocks in the Sherman Mountains. JEFF GNASS
Above: The rugged country of Laramie Peak. LORRAINE G. BONNEY

The Gangplank of the Laramie Range, crossed by Interstate 80.
D.E. TRIMBLE, U.S. GEOLOGICAL SURVEY

somehow escaped exhumation when the rest of the Tertiary blanket covering the Laramie Range and the high plains was cleared away. This narrow finger of Miocene rock on the east flank of the Laramie Range extends from the high plains up to the Precambrian crest of the range.

More important, having escaped the fate of the rest of the Miocene sediments, the Gangplank is the only place between Mexico and Canada where a Miocene surface (once buried the Laramie Range) still is in contact with the granite core of a mountain summit. Because I-80 and the Union Pacific cross this narrow finger, one can step off this intact bit of Great Plains onto a Rocky Mountain summit.

From the Gangplank is seen the red sandstone Paleozoics that once extended in a continuous sheet across the area. The sheet, mountains included, was uplifted, then erosion stripped the summit areas down to their Precambrian cores, leaving "islands" of Paleozoic rock along the mountain flanks. These were ultimately buried and then partly exhumed from the alluvial debris that spread eastward, in giant fans, from the Laramie Range summits onto the Great Plains. Today the eroded forms of the tilted Paleozoic sediments along the flanks of these ranges are called "hogbacks." Sediments at the Gangplank, however, still cover these forms, making a smooth graded

surface where the Union Pacific laid tracks over the first major barrier to transportation west of the Mississippi.

After the half-mile-long Gangplank, I-80 travels on the Precambrian core of pink granite to the summit at 8,816', highest point on I-80 between the Atlantic and Pacific.

Originally a buffalo trail the Indians followed across the range to hunting grounds in the Medicine Bows, the Gangplank was accidentally discovered by whites in 1865. Major General Grenville Dodge and his crew were searching the area for a Union Pacific route across the Rockies and surprised a Sioux war party that escaped by this route. Their path showed Dodge the one spot in the whole Rocky Mountain front that connects the Great Plains to the mountain summits without requiring a tunnel or a switchbacking road. It simplified the building of the Union Pacific and thus the settlement of the Northwest.

Harry Yount, namesake of Younts Peak in the Teton Wilderness, had a close call when he found a bears' den in the Laramie Mountains. Expecting only one bear, he failed to have ball and powder ready to reload. But there were three bears in the den—and Yount set new records in reloading his weapon. A tenacious hunter, Yount followed one huge bear, "Old Big Foot," for six or seven years before bringing him down in the Laramie Range. The bear weighed 1,600 pounds.

The Laramie Range has numerous small caves in its thin limestones. Table Mountain Cave, on private property, has a date of 1841 carved on its walls. In the small Horned Owl cave on the southern west flank were found late Pleistocene animal remains. The Bates Creek Ice Cave at the north end of the west flank has permanent ice accumulations that might prove to be remnants of Pleistocene climate. Diamond exploration is being done in the southern Laramie Range in the Iron Mountain Exploration District. The number of diamonds found so far is not significant; the grade, size and quality are.

The Sherman Mountains
Some 40 million years ago nature flung a handful of granite on the Laramie plains, scraps from the building of the Rocky Mountains, and formed the Sherman Mountains—according to Indian legend. The rocks, weathered by the elements, took on weird shapes. Lovely glens, sites of ancient rites, have been used through the ages by Indians and whites alike.

In 1924 an English professor at the University of Wyoming, Mabelle DeKay, christened the area Vedauwoo, from the Arapahoe wording meaning "earthborn." Civilian Conservation Corps workers built picnic tables and fireplaces during the '30s and constructed a still-usable trail to the top of Friction Tower.

The ever fascinating Blair-Vedauwoo rocks are one of several clusters found in the Sherman Mountains at the south end of the Laramie Range, 35 miles west of Cheyenne and 15 miles east of Laramie, just north of I-80. Other groups are Elephants Head and Raggedtop. All former Indian campsites, they are remnants of the crest of the Laramie Range that was not eroded during the Late Tertiary time. This pygmy mountain group (their highest point is only some 750' above the ground) are blocky towers of weathered Sherman granite consisting of the crystalline fragments of feldspar and quartz originally found in granite. They cover the landscape in many places, and their "rotten" granite can easily be dug by a hand shovel. They are typical of granite batholiths that, upon cooling from the molten state, contract and crack in giant rectangular joint systems. They are characterized by their lack of cracks and holds, providing wonderful friction and chimney climbs. The 300' vertical climb of Walts Wall, for instance, is rated one of the best technical climbs in North America. These rocks rise 200' to 300' above their evergreen-sprinkled bases.

Among the striking aspects of the geology here are the large, rounded, balanced rocks seen on the skyline, some of which are as large as a house. Such rocks were originally bounded by fracture planes that divided the entire rock mass into rough, rectangular blocks. Weathering has enlarged the fractures and cracks, removed some of the original granite, and left behind the individual blocks. Grit-laden winds have helped to round off the blocks and give them mushroom shapes.

The Snowy and Medicine Bow Ranges

The special quality of the Snowy Range-Medicine Bow Range, a doubly named, double level range, is discovered by driving west from Laramie on U.S. Highway 130. From the flats of the dry Laramie Basin, the road spirals into higher elevations where, in a matter of a few miles, the visitor is above timberline in the compressed but startling world of classic alpine beauty. Glacial ice originating in the Snowy Range carved out the stunning east

Summer sunset in the Vedauwoo Rocks. JEFF GNASS

French Creek in the Medicine Bow Mountains. JEFF GNASS

face and the glacial basins at the base, then the prominent glaciers slipped down the northward slopes that are now characterized by hundreds of small ponds and lakes. From cacti and horned toads found in the basins, to the arctic tundra and ptarmigan at the top of Medicine Bow Peak, changes in flora, fauna and scenery result from the 5,000' difference in elevation and rainfall.

The double-levelled Medicine Bow Range is characterized by a rather broad, flat 9,000' meadowed plateau that was warped out of the earth's crust with a fold on the west and a splitting fault on the east. The top was then levelled to a peneplain by erosive forces, which, failing to carve away the quartzite, left 1,000' faceted scarp slopes on the east. At the base lie many small glacial lakes of considerable charm.

The quartzite of the "Snowy Range," including Medicine Bow Peak itself (12,006'), is as crystalline as cube sugar. The maximum level of the Miocene blanket that covered Wyoming is clearly marked by timberline, at 10,000', where the white quartzite "Snowy" crest rests on the plateau. In a matter of only 10 million years, the range was thrust up by the Laramide Orogeny, stripped of its sedimentary load, and thrust eastward a few miles. The rock in front was rumpled like a tablecloth, forming folds with anticlines that trapped what would one day be oil.

Few areas in the United States contain as complete a geologic record as the Medicine Bow Mountains. The broad-fold uplift exposed old Precambrian rocks, gneisses and schists, quartzites and slates, about 2.5+-billion-years-old. Here are the greatest variety of rocks of Precambrian age and the most complete section of metasedimentary rocks known in Wyoming. The only fossils found in Wyoming's Precambrians, *stromatolites,* are some of the oldest known forms of life found, a type of marine algae (seaweed) that lived in reefs some 2 billion years ago.

Two tiny wilderness areas have been established at the south end of the Medicine Bow Mountains. The 15,260-acre Savage Run Wilderness, the first to be established (by Rep. Teno Roncalio, in 1978), contains the potential 950-acre Lodgepole Pine Research Natural Area. Savage Run was the only major unlogged drainage on the whole west slope of this range. With its big old trees, it is a favorite recreational area. A public hearing held for it at Saratoga in 1978, with free beer for everybody, served by Mr. Roncalio himself, is a day remembered by many.

In 1984 the Wyoming Wilderness Act established the 22,363-acre North Platte River Canyon Wilderness. It included the thrilling whitewater of North Gate Canyon, a 13.5-mile segment of the North Platte, plus important bighorn and elk habitat and a nationally famous trout fishery. The BLM's l,099-acre Prospect Mountain Wilderness Study Area, with its diversity of topography, wildlife and vegetative zones, would complement this wilderness area, but it failed to be approved. Its outstanding tree and plant qualities, spectacular scenery, interesting geological outcrops and pinnacles all make it a worthy addition to the wilderness system.

The 771-acre Snowy Range Research Natural Area was designated in 1935 to study old-growth Engelmann spruce stands. The de facto wilderness in this area failed to become official.

The Art Fawcett Never Never Wilderness Area, otherwise known as the Laramie Peak Roadless Area, composed of 30,000 acres in two units, had tremendous public support because of the years of work by Fawcett, but the Forest Service did not select it for wilderness status because of the commercial potential of the ponderosa.

No national forest suffered the impact of a decade of clearcutting in the '60s more than the Medicine Bow National Forest. The Medicine Bows may be one of the most abused mountain ranges in the country. Almost the entire range, except for the Snowy Range, is a mass of checkerboard timber cuts. It has 24 remaining roadless areas that are among the forest's most popular hiking, fishing, hunting and camping spots. In the forest plan, the Forest Service proposed allowing intensive logging in 12 of the areas. Oil and gas development and other mineral development activities will be allowed in most of the remaining roadless areas, driving out elk, hikers and others.

Ed Haggarty, a poor sheepherder, found some red clay near Bridger Peak in the Sierra Madre Range one day in 1896. It turned out to be 70-percent-pure copper and the start of the Rudefeha, later Ferris-Haggarty, Mine. After 1,220 tons were freighted to the Union Pacific by four-horse teams, the boom started. It supported 5,000 miners working in three shifts, earning $3 for an eight-hour shift. Other towns sprang up and, by 1903, besides Encampment there were Rudefeha, Dillon, where "there ain't no night," Rambler and Copperton. At one time the largest copper mine in the world, the Ramburg, was here. The most publicized, the Ferris–Haggerty, led to the founding of the town of Grand Encampment, so named for the fur-trading rendezvous held from 1840 to 1851. The longest aerial tram in the world was built over the mountains from the mine to Encampment (the Grand had been dropped) at a cost of $350,000. It was powered by four wood-burning stations. A railroad spur line was built from Walcott to Encampment, by then called the "Pittsburgh of the West," but the copper bubble burst in 1910 when the U.S. Railroad and Copper Co. was indicted for fraudulent sales of stocks and went bankrupt.

Called the Sierra Madre in Wyoming and the Park Range in Colorado, this small finger of mountain crest carries the Continental Divide from the Great Divide Basin southward across the state line. Quite similar to the Medicine Bows geologically, it lacks the broad plateau surface of the latter and is composed of metamorphosed sedimentary rocks that have been intruded by ore-bearing juices. Gold, silver, and other metals were found in small quantities in Precambrian crystalline and metamorphic rocks.

Jeep roads, ghost-town exploration, hunting, fishing and ski touring are the thrills of this Continental Divide range that rises west of Encampment and just north of the Colorado-Wyoming border. Its rounded forested peaks rise from 9,000' to 11,004' on Bridger Peak. It is famous range and dude-ranching country. The great copper rush with its boom towns proclaimed a brief glory we remember today in creaking ruins, forlorn graveyards and "boot hills." This once jealously-guarded Indian hunting ground was found by Henry Fraeb and his 35 trappers searching for beaver in 1841. A skirmish left five dead, including Fraeb and resulted in the naming of Battle Mountain, lake and creek.

The town of Battle, perched on the Continental Divide along the twisting road up from Encampment, was an overnight freighting stop. Two miles west was Battle Lake where Thomas A. Edison, a member of the Henry Draper solar eclipse expedition of 1878, went fishing. When his bamboo fishing rod became entangled in a tree, he discovered the toughness of bamboo fibers. This led him to conceive of using non-conducting filaments for the incandescent electric light. There's a monument here to his dream.

The Huston Park Wilderness Area, 50,000 acres of lovely

open mountain parks and forest mosaic, straddles the Sierra Madre Range. A 40-acre sphagnum bog, adjacent to Red Mountain, is in this wilderness. As a natural history area, it would be used to study plants in a peat-bog environment.

The Encampment River Wilderness, 10,400 acres, protects the river's free-flowing 11-mile segment where bighorn sheep and mountain lions inhabit the steep canyon walls. The upper Colorado segment of the river has been recommended for protected status.

The BLM named a 3,380-acre Encampment River Canyon Wilderness Study Area that did not achieve wilderness status. The unit, in the Sierra Madre foothills, included the Encampment River and Miner Creek canyons, both of which are deep, spectacular gorges, with diverse vegetation that furnishes crucial winter habitat for deer, elk and bighorn sheep. Rock outcrops and steep talus slopes are abundant, giving the unit a rough, wild appearance.

Stream-washed crystalline quartzite of the Snowy Range at the outlet of Lake Marie. The climbing cliffs of Medicine Bow Peak behind.
JEFF GNASS

NORTH CENTRAL RANGES

Pack train in the Bighorn Mountains.
GEORGE WUERTHNER

Marion Lake in Cloud Peak Wilderness. GEORGE WUERTHNER

The Bighorn Range

The Bighorn Range, with the Cloud Peak Wilderness Area at its heart, is like a fragile island in a snarling sea, an oasis in a savage desert. Staunchly defended by the Crow Indians as hunting and religious grounds, the Bighorns were the scene of many bloody battles. Today's battles are over the integrity of the Bighorns, which face strangulation by roads, people and industry.

Isolated in the heart of the industrial northeast of Wyoming, the Bighorns offer wilderness with granite summits and timbered slopes, and are surrounded by the billowing sagebrush plains of Powder River Basin on the east and the Bighorn Basin on the west—two storehouses of coal, oil and uranium, whose manufactures have voracious water habits.

Like a waning half moon, the Bighorns sweep westward in a great arc. From southern Montana around the Bighorn Basin, they taper westward as lower, less rugged rolling upland,to link with the Owl Creek Mountains in a more or less continuous chain. The highest, most rugged part of the range lies west of Buffalo, where the mountain front soars abruptly to spectacular Cloud Peak (13,167').

The range was venerated by the Sioux, Crow and Cheyenne tribes who journeyed into its solitude to find their inspiration. Here is one of the great mysteries of the aboriginal past—the great "Medicine Wheel"—built so long ago that even legendary history is lacking. Also in the area are numerous caves. In fact, the Madison limestone and Bighorn dolomite flanks of the range are riddled with more than a hundred caves of assorted sizes, depths and lengths. The well explored Tongue River Cave is the most visited and most easily located. Some caves have "permanent ice" and two, Dead Man Cave and South Fork Ice Cave, may be neo-glacial remnants. The ice caves have been used since primitive times (often by poachers) as natural freezers.

The Bighorns also have long been a favorite of geologists. Geology professors bring their students to the Bighorns to see its Precambrian rocks, the oldest in the world, and the exposures that show the chain of geologic events. The bluffs along Paint Rock Creek at the west end of the wilderness area contain exposures of the colorful sedimentary rocks deposited in ancient seas. The oldest known fossil vertebrates in the world, of primitive armored jawless fish, are found in the range.

One hundred twenty miles long, and from 30 to 50 miles wide, the Bighorns are geologically divided into three segments. They are the result of a two-episode uplift of the Laramide Orogeny, and a classic example of a ramp uplift. The granitic-gneissic core was upthrust vertically about 25,000' at Cloud Peak, with a slight thrust eastward near the center and a slight counterthrust westward in the northern and southern sections of the range, a twist characteristic of this range. The uplift, one of the last of the Laramide Orogeny, is asymmetrical, but not constantly so—the north and south ends are steeper on the west and the central section has its steep side facing the deep structural Powder River Basin on the east flank. Unlike the topsy-turvy tilts of warps, faults and folds in other ranges, there was little tilting in the Bighorns except at their margins. Secondary faults occurred later. The lift heaved and threw off the overlying crust of sedimentaries that had draped themselves along the flanks of the range, forming them around the granite as foothills.

The Medicine Wheel was first discovered by white men in 1880. Crow legend says it was built "by people who had no iron." The general shape resembles the Sun Dance lodge of the Plains Indians. Mystery still shrouds the builders and their purposes. RON MAMOT

91

Like the Wind River Range, the glacier-carved gneissic heart of the Bighorns is well hidden from roadside views except for Cloud Peak rising above the foothills near the middle of the range, and the distant glimpses one gets of the Bighorn giants—Penrose, Sawtooth, Hallalujah and Black Tooth, with many beautiful parks between—which are best seen from Red Grade Road out of Bighorn west to Burgess.

Until you've hiked some five to 15 miles into the heart of the range, you won't see its truly alpine nature, the sharp summits, sheer rock faces that overshadow glacier-cut valleys, the still-active glaciated heart that is largely undisturbed. Here the gneissic rocks rise in sharp ridges above the plateau to peaks of 12,000' to 13,000' elevations including Cloud Peak (13,167') and Black Tooth (12,960').

Classic glacial cirques were formed here, with preglacial valleys spaced far enough apart to permit each glacier to

operate independently. The climate was mild enough to prevent glaciation of the divides, yet homogeneous rocks allowed the glaciers on both sides of a mountain to gnaw their way into the rock at the same rate. There were favorable vertical cleavage and little crumbling or erosion after the glaciers receded. Thus, interestingly, and seldom found in other glaciated mountains, the preglacial surface was preserved along many of the crests. There are numerous little lakes scooped out of granite basins or dammed by moraines, many not even connected by streams. Several small glaciers exist, the largest one still working on Cloud Peak's east face. The headwaters of the Bighorn, Tongue and North Fork Powder rivers rise in this range. With 300 small glacier-fed lakes, 800 miles of trout streams, and 3,000 acres of trout-stocked lakes, it's a fisherman's paradise. However, wildlife sightings in the wilderness are very rare.

The 137,000-acre Cloud Peak Primitive Area became

Cloud Peak Wilderness Area, with the addition of 57,500 acres in 1984. Of the 17 RARE II roadless areas that qualified for wilderness status, none was so designated in the Wyoming Wilderness Act. No mountain range had such excellent wilderness potential as the Bighorns, but they ended up as the classical "wilderness on the rocks," a beautiful hunk of rock up along the crest. None of the magnificent wildlife habitat was included—the valuable winter range and calving areas—those fringes where the lower slopes break into quaking aspen country and sagebrush grasslands. Virtually all the lower slopes that had any forest or meadow were released to the Forest Service.

It was due to Rep. John Seiberling (D-OH) that Cloud Peak got the additional acreage. He was able to add 37,000 acres to the north end of the wilderness, but unable to save the exceptional Rock Creek area. He described a sense of loss in commenting on the compro-

Left: Black Tooth is on the right, with Woolsey the sharp spire to the left; Kearney Creek in the foreground. WILLIAM R. NELSON
Above: "Fallen City" along U.S. Highway 14. Rocks broke loose and the earth's crust buckled in lowering of Powder River Basin and rising of Bighorn Range some 60 million years ago. KENT & DONNA DANNEN

Facing page, left: Hunt mountain, Bighorn National Forest. JEFF GNASS
Right: North Powder River in the Bighorns east of Lovell. TOM DIETRICH

mise bill: "I would have preferred to see the additions in the Rock Creek area [which] runs all the way from alpine tundra down through scenic canyons to the edge of the prairie, and represents the only real opportunity to have the proposed wilderness incorporate a vast spectrum of ecological systems...I was very impressed with its rugged, scenic terrain, dramatic rock spires, and beautiful canyons. Unfortunately, much of the area has been leased for oil and gas and the [Wyoming] delegation was unwilling to designate it as wilderness or wilderness study at this time. It would be my hope, however, that if the area's oil and gas potential proves to be low that a future Congress would reconsider the wilderness option for this beautiful and fragile area. In the meanwhile we would ask that the Forest Service exercise special sensitivity in planning for management of the area and...any oil and gas exploration activities on the existing leases be conducted by helicopter...The Subcommittee has received a great deal of input from Wyoming residents asking that the roadless nature of the Rock Creek area be protected..."

Long overhunted, the Bighorns' elk herd had dwindled to 30 animals by 1900. Transplants were made from Jackson Hole and Yellowstone, which pays off in good hunting now. The eastside UM Ranch on the east side, with traditional and natural winter range for hundreds of elk, was deeded to Wyoming Game and Fish, and is now the Bud Love Big Game Winter Refuge.

If the Forest Service had built all the roads proposed in their early-1986 draft management plan, at no time would a person be more than 375 yards from a road, anywhere on the forest (excluding the wilderness area, of course). This caused a public uproar, especially in Sheridan and Buffalo, and the Forest Service proposed a Final Plan that included slightly less roading.

The public succeeded in getting the timber-cut decreased from 21.1 million board feet (mbf) by the year 2030, to 16.5 mbf, and the almost 2,500 miles of new and reconstructed roads reduced to 1,000 miles, closed but for a few miles.

The Owl Creek Range
Swinging westward off the southern tail of the Bighorns is the Owl Creek Range, loosely linking the Bighorns to the southern end of the Washakie-Absaroka Range and forming the southern boundary of the Bighorn Basin. Synclines separate it from the Washakies on the west and the

Left: The "Hoodoos/Badlands" of Bobcat Draw Wilderness Study Area. Bottom left: The Natural Trap Cave has been trapping animals for more than 20,000 years and perhaps since about 100,000 years ago. The serially deposited and clearly stratified animal remains found in this 85' karst sinkhole in Madison limestone document environmental changes during and since the last full glacial advance.
Right: Rare finds from the Natural Trap Cave include these (left to right) skulls of the North American lion and American cheetah, and tooth of a mammoth. Other fossil bones found have been of wolf, woodland musk ox, pronghorn antelope, short-face bear, Pleistocene camel, bighorn sheep, wolverine, pine marten and horse.
BUREAU OF LAND MANAGEMENT PHOTOS

Facing page: Porcupine Falls in the Bighorns. CHARLES KAY

Bighorns on the east, making it structurally distinct. It is also distinctive in that it is thrust southward, not east or west as with most Wyoming ranges. Like the Washakie Range, its west end was buried by the Absaroka Range.

It is a series of tilted blocks, anticlines in echelon, which trend northwest even though the range as a whole, both topographically and structurally, trends to the west. It has a gentle slope to the north and escarpments and a major

Big Goose Park in the Bighorns. GEORGE WUERTHNER

fracture bounding the south side. Predominantly in the Wind River Indian Reservation, it has plenty of superb alpine grassland that has been extensively overgrazed. This once-great habitat also has been overhunted.

Although the Absarokas to the west make this range appear small, its highest points rise 2,000' above the basin at the head of Owl Creek canyon, and 3,000' above the northern margin of Wind River Basin. The Owl Creeks have a granitic core covered with limestone and sandstone. This arid country, sparsely vegetated with sagebrush, grass and a thick juniper cover, culminates in Phlox Mountain (9,684') near the west end. Gold and copper have been found on Birdseye and Copper Mountains (8,053') in the east end.

The Bureau of Land Management's Copper Mountain Wilderness Study Area is a little gem perched above the northeast corner of Boysen Reservoir, 6,858 acres of rough topography—steep-sided canyons, rocky sloped peaks, numerous geological formations and outcrops— that still has many pristine ecological communities and great views of the Wind River Range, Beaver Rim and Boysen Reservoir.

The traveler taking U.S. Highway 20 from Thermopolis to Shoshoni can see how the Wind River has cut its huge 2,240'-deep channel through the Owl Creek Range, severing west from east so completely that the eastern section is often considered a different range, and is known locally as the Bridger Mountains. Still, it's all part of the same uplift.

The Wind River, hugged by U.S. Highway 20, flows north across these mountains in a magnificent canyon. The canyon walls tower more than 3,000' above the river and in them is seen a spectacular cross-section of the mountain range geology. Interpretive signs along the highway add to the visitor's understanding.

The Owl Creek Range is one of the many ranges of folded rocks developed during Laramide time. Its core of Precambrian crystalline and metamorphic rocks, is clearly exposed in Wind River Canyon. Hung on this Precambrian core on the north and south sides of the range are the Paleozoic and Mesozoic sediments.

The Owl Creeks are broadly asymmetrical, their southern

margin overturned toward the Wind River Basin with much large-scale block and thrust faulting, while the northern part of the range dips gently into the Big Horn Basin. Outliers of Early Tertiary strata occur atop the Owl Creek divide in many places, remnants of the extensive sheet of rocks that almost completely buried the mountains prior to the secondary uplift and erosion.

The geologic history of the superimposed Wind River is fascinating. The ancestral Wind River was established on the Early Tertiary blanket of high fill, laid down by the Absaroka volcanoes that covered the Owl Creeks and surrounding basins. Rising in the mountains around Dubois, the river flowed southeast to Riverton, where today it makes an abrupt northward bend. At this point, the river was captured and diverted by a north-flowing tributary of the Bighorn River. A widespread general uplift in later Tertiary times rejuvenated the Wind River.

As the fill was excavated in very late Cenozoic time, the Wind River, which had inherited this course across the mountains, cut and continued to develop the Wind River Canyon. Called the Wind River in the Wind River Basin but the Bighorn in the Bighorn Basin, it's the same river. Where they join in Wind River Canyon is called the Wedding of the Waters. More than 420 million years of earth's history are represented in the canyon.

The Wind River Canyon was so precipitous that it presented a real barrier to travel down the river. Early-day freighters had to forge primitive roads across the range over several passes (Bridger and DePass east of the river, Mexican and Merrit west of the river). These roads still are undeveloped and primitive.

Near the south base of the Owls, on the Wind River Indian Reservation some 26 miles northwest of Shoshoni, lies the small Twin Buttes Fossil Area, an extensively dissected region of badlands. As a result of downfolding near a deep trough axis of the Wind River structural basin, remnants of the highly fossiliferous layer from Early Tertiary time (the Shotgun Member [layer] of the Fort Union Formation of the Paleocene epoch) missed removal by erosion. Discovered in 1959 by the U.S. Geological Survey, it is one of the most important fossil sites of Paleocene age in North America and contains a

highly diversified mammalian fauna including extremely rare primates. Thousands of fossil teeth and jaw fragments have been recovered from the area by the Smithsonian Institution, University of Wyoming and Harvard University. The amazing fact that many animal fossils, believed to represent two separate Paleocene ages, occur together here presents an enigma that may well call for redefinitions of many Paleocene ages.

Left: Banded blue and red mudstone on the Wind River Reservation. KENT & DONNA DANNEN *Above: Petroglyph in the Owl Creek Range.* R. BARRY

THE NORTHEAST CORNER

Pronghorn antelope.
JEFF & PAT VANUGA

Sunrise on Devils Tower, viewed from the southeast. JEFF GNASS

Bear Lodge Mountains and Devils Tower

Wyoming's boundaries include the short end of the broad domal uplift called the Black Hills in South Dakota, where most of them are located. In Wyoming, they are known as the Bear Lodge Mountains. Although Wyoming's portion of the Black Hills is small, it features the fascinating Devils Tower, the fluted monolith of volcanic plug that has captured the human imagination since earliest times.

The Indians called the area Mateo Tepee (Mato Tipi) meaning Bears' Lodge, because furrows between the Tower's vertical polygonal columns looked like scratches made by bears' claws.

The natural landmark, which resembles a colossal petrified tree stump, received its modern name from Col. Richard I. Dodge, commander of a military escort for a U.S. survey party to the area in 1875. He called the strange formation Devils Tower from an Indian name that meant "Bad God's Tower." This 865' monolith towers 1,280' above the Belle Fourche River, the tallest such formation in the United States. From its 1,000'-wide base it tapers to 275' at its flat summit. The rock, similar to granite but with less quartz is known as phonolite porphyry (phono, the musical ring of rock when struck; porphyry, the rock texture, large conspicuous crystals of white feldspar in a fine gray groundmass). The curious and characteristic fluted appearance is due to joints having formed (like drying mud cracks) while it was completely buried, solidifying from hot, liquid form. Such joints are hexagonal and, usually, vertical, since they are oriented perpendicularly to the cooling surface, which in this case was earth's surface. Several such formations are found on the fringes of the Black Hills.

As the easternmost extension of the Rocky Mountain chain, the Black Hills are the youngest of the Laramide progeny. With little fanfare and no major thrust faults, they bulged up in the extreme northwest corner of South Dakota, spilling over into Wyoming's northeast corner. Billion-year-old Precambrian schists and granites were pushed into an egg-shaped anticlinal uplift. These intruded into the overlying sedimentary layers, doming them up, fragmenting and pushing them aside, where they encircled and outlined the highland of Precambrian rock in concentric rings of resistant sandstone and limestone ridges and slabs. Most of this happened in South

1937 painting of Mato Tipi by Herbert A. Collins, located in the Visitors' Center, Devils Tower National Monument.
RON MAMOT PHOTO

Dakota's Black Hills, with Wyoming's Bear Lodge Mountains section getting very little of the Precambrian rock. The Black Hills escaped glaciation and at the end of the Ice Age looked about as they do now.

Devils Tower is a classic core of igneous intrusion. Geologist Henry Newton, under escort by Col. Dodge's party, provided the first written description of it, "an obelisk of trachyte, with a columnar structure...[that] is entirely inaccessible." In the throes of the Laramide Orogeny during Eocene time, magma or molten rock material welled

up in scattered locations in the Black Hills area from a deep-seated magma chamber into a sedimentary formation of the earth's crust. At some places magma broke through the surface. At others, the magma was unable to break through the overlying sedimentary crust and slowly cooled underground, crystallizing into phonolite porphyry. In the following eóns, the sedimentary cover was stripped from the intrusion by erosion. Thousands of feet of rock thus were removed from the magma intrusions.

The Missouri Buttes

Nearby Inyan Kara Mountain and the four Missouri Buttes are similar intrusive structures. When looking at Devils Tower from U.S. Highway 14, you may think the Buttes are right next to it, but they are actually several miles beyond. Although included in the original proposal for a national monument, they are now on private property. They have sheer faces but gentle slopes make their summits easily accessible. The Missouri Buttes and Devils Tower drew molten rock from the same magma chamber far underground. Devils Tower welled up into a bedding plane of the Jurassic Sundance Formation. The small amounts of igneous debris at the base of these structures indicate that erosion didn't remove much of the igneous rock composing Devils Tower; the original igneous masses were about the same size as today.

Downcutting by the Belle Fourche River cleaned off the sedimentary cover of Devils Tower, exhuming it more efficiently than the Buttes which were farther from the river. Weathering and erosion has been a two-stage process. The top 150 yards of Devils Tower, exposed much longer, is in a greater weathered state, its cracks and joints much more prominent than the lower part.

Devils Tower was the nation's first National Monument (1,266 acres, designated by President Theodore Roosevelt in 1906). It was first climbed as part of the Fourth of July picnic celebration in 1893. Two local ranchers, Bill Rogers and Willard Ripley, drove long wooden pegs into a crack between two of the columns, bracing them with an outer vertical support to form a 350' ladder. At the summit, the two men patriotically unfurled the American flag, which the wind blew to the ground. Pieces of it were sold as souvenirs to the crowd of 1,000. The ranchers' precarious ladder was used for 20 years by other aspirants to the summit. In 1937 Fritz Wiessner, Lawrence Coveney and Bill House used rope, strength

Cottonwoods and pink sandstone above the Belle Fourche River.
GEORGE WUERTHNER

Facing page: Red Butte in the Black Hills. The red Spearfish formation is protected by the white gypsum cap.
KENT & DONNA DANNEN

and skill to climb the seemingly impossible fluted columns of the great southeast face in four hours and 46 minutes. In the publicity stunt of 1941, George Hopkins landed by parachute on the summit on October 7, expecting to be there only a short time. He was thwarted from descending when the hundreds of feet of rope, tossed down to him from a plane, became a nightmare of twisted, knotted coils. After a frustrating six days, and several failed rescue attempts, he was daringly rescued under appalling conditions of ice and rain by Jack Durrance, Paul Petzoldt, Merrill McLane, Henry Coulter and others.

Despite the publicity, the monument had very few visitors until the release of the movie *Close Encounters of the Third Kind,* in which friendly aliens land atop Devils Tower. Then, the number of visitors doubled.

GLOSSARY

The photos on these two pages are of some of the best known climbers in the Tetons including Glenn Exum and Dick Pownall completing an ascent of the north face of the Grand Teton.
FRIEDMAN PHOTOS

Andesitic lava—Gray, fine-grained volcanic rock.

Anticline—A rock structure in which layered rocks dip away from a central crest or axis in opposite directions, like the roof of a house.

Arch—A broad regional anticline; regional upbowing of sedimentary strata.

Basalt—An extrusive igneous rock, black in color, common rock in lava flows.

Basin—A topographic basin is an area of lower elevation surrounded by a rim of higher ground; often found in eroded core of an anticline. A structural basin is a synclinal area; all strata dip toward the deeper part; may be regional in extent.

Batholith—Masses of granitic rock having a surface area of 40 square miles or more are called batholiths. Smaller masses are called stocks.

Bedding—Sedimentary rocks which occur in layers are said to be bedded; layering.

Breccia—A rock made of sharp fragments embedded in material that was once sand or clay, included volcanic mud

Caldera—A crater much larger than the volcanic vent that formed it when the volcano's center collapsed

Cirque—Bow-shaped erosional form at the head of valleys that have been or currently are occupied by alpine glaciers. Walls are very steep, and the profile across the valley is U-shaped.

Conglomerate—A sedimentary rock composed of rounded to angular detrital fragments of pre-existing rocks surrounded by a matrix of smaller grain size. The larger particles range upward from 2 mm. diameter.

Dike—A tabular-shaped body of igneous rock that cuts across (intrudes) the structure of adjacent rocks.

Dome—A special form of anticline which approximates a circular pattern in map view.

Era—Geologic periods are grouped together into larger time units called eras.

Extrusive rock—When a silicate melt called magma reaches the surface and solidifies, the resulting rocks are called extrusive rocks.

Fault (normal and reverse)—A displacement of rocks in the earth's crust along a fracture.

Granite—A common igneous rock characterized by the presence of free quartz, orthoclase, feldspar, and minor accessory minerals such as biotite, hornblende and magnetite.

Igneous—The word derived from the Latin word for fire and is used as an adjective. Igneous rocks are those which result from the consolidation of molten silicate melts.

Intrusive rock—Rocks which have been formed by the consolidation of magma at depth below the surface of the earth. The rocks are usually crystalline—that is,